# CROWN AND GOWN

An Illustrated History of the University of Aberdeen
1495 - 1995

The cover design by Victor E Davidson is based on the earliest surviving painting of King's College dating from around 1640.

# CROWN
# AND
# GOWN
## 1495 - 1995

**An Illustrated History of the University of Aberdeen**

Jennifer J Carter and Colin A McLaren

Designed by Victor E Davidson

ABERDEEN UNIVERSITY PRESS

First published 1994
Aberdeen University Press
(c) University of Aberdeen 1994

**British Library Cataloguing in Publication Data**

A catalogue record of this book is
available from the British Library

ISBN 1 85752 240 0 (pbk)

Printed by BPC–AUP Ltd. Aberdeen

# Foreword
by the Chancellor of the University of Aberdeen

*Sir Kenneth Alexander,*
*BSc (Econ), LLD, DUniv,*
*FEIS, FBEcScot, FRSE.*

TO SURVEY the five hundred years of a university's history in a short book is a challenging, even daunting, task, and I am extremely pleased to report that Jennifer Carter and Colin McLaren have met that challenge with distinction. Beginning when scholars believed in invariable laws of nature which had little or no empirical basis, the University of Aberdeen has contributed, through both teaching and research, to a better understanding and the development of freedom of thought and invention. *Crown and Gown* presents an overview of the life of the university, influenced by and influencing the spiritual, intellectual, political and social life of the surrounding world, of Scotland and in particular the North of Scotland for which the University has been and remains the centre of learning.

The initial vision, linked to perceived educational needs in the late fifteenth century, is radically different five hundred years later, but the founder's careful attention to detail in finance, curricula and in the duties of both teachers and students remain as elements equally essential to the success of a modern university. The importance of intellectual and academic innovation is a constant requirement, most interestingly illustrated in this history. The pioneering extra-mural work in the dissemination of scientific understanding raises the contemporary issue of how far universities have failed to develop this important role.

Readers in the late twentieth century will be interested in the dramatic swings in the fortune of the university, but must not let recent history confirm them in the view that history repeats itself. The widely different circumstances of these swings denies rather than confirms such a popular misconception. Looking for continuities beyond the academic pillars on which a successful university must be built I would single out European connections as being of considerable and now growing significance. With Paris and Bologna as the early founding exemplars, it is appropriate that Aberdeen has recently made a significant contribution to student exchanges within the European Union.

The history outlined in this book is so rich and varied that readers will want to add to their initial enlightenment by returning to specific aspects, perhaps when a contemporary issue raises the possibility of comparisons with the past. I congratulate the University of Aberdeen on having such a good story to tell and the authors for telling it so well.

*Kenneth Alexander.*

*1 King's College and Old Aberdeen in 1878, by W E Lockhart. A serene setting for the 'hard grinding' and 'wild vagaries' described in Neil Maclean's* Life at a Northern University.

*2 King's College and Old Aberdeen around 1820, by Francis Oliver Finch, showing how the rural surroundings of King's survived into the nineteenth century. Still the 'pleasant well situated and retired village' which had housed the university since its earliest days.*

# 1 Foundations, 1495–1593

3

3 *The crown surmounting the tower of King's College Chapel was modelled on that of the Holy Roman Emperor. It was probably intended as a graceful compliment to King James IV, patron and benefactor of the university, symbolising his claim to imperial authority within the realm.*

4 *George Thomson's inscription on the base of the reconstructed crown and lantern.*

ON THURSDAY 7 February 1633 a great snowstorm swept across Scotland. A gale struck the chapel tower of King's College in Old Aberdeen, toppled the crown that had adorned it for over a hundred years and sent the supporting masonry crashing through the chapel roof. The staff of the college inspected the damage in dismay. The crown was 'a goodly ornament', 'a royal monument'; it must, they agreed, be restored at once. To that end, said John Forbes, professor of divinity, 'they did carefully employ both their purses and their pains'. Finding their own purses were not deep enough, they set up an appeal, raising funds from the citizens of the neighbouring town of New Aberdeen, the local lairds and the nobility, and by the following year had collected enough to employ George Thomson, 'an excellent mason of singular device'. But their troubles were not over: the money ran out and Thomson stopped work. Only when the town council of New Aberdeen came to the rescue with a generous grant did he resume, rebuilding the four arched ribs and the eight-sided lantern and setting above them a copy of the fallen crown. His handiwork still stands, inscribed on the west face with his name.

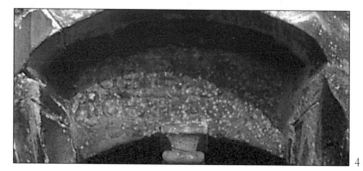

4

This story of the crown symbolises the story of the university over the past five hundred years. All the ingredients are there. The remote academic community, proud of its heritage; a sudden crisis, made worse by shortage of funds; a determined response, reinforced by local support; and in the end, triumph over adversity. During the three centuries in which King's

College and Marischal College existed side by side, and in the century and more since they were fused into the present University of Aberdeen, the plot has been repeated time and time again. Yet the university has done more than simply survive. In the face of political and religious upheaval, social and economic change, it has maintained its commitment to the pursuit of learning and it has made a significant contribution to the life of the region, the nation and the wider world.

The 'University and King's College' was founded in 1495 by William Elphinstone, Bishop of Aberdeen. He was then in his early sixties and an eminent figure in church and state. A career churchman from the start, he had studied canon (or church) law at the universities of Glasgow and Paris, and civil law at Orleans. But his interests went well beyond the cramped columns of legal treatises: at Paris he was drawn to the work of the early humanists – scholars who were rediscovering the literature of Greece and Rome and using it to reinterpret their own world. Back in Scotland, he took his place on the council of James III, serving the king as a judge of appeals, as ambassador to the courts of England and France, and – briefly – as chancellor, before the reign ended in chaos in 1488. That year, he was consecrated Bishop of Aberdeen: portrayed later in his episcopal robes, he looks surprisingly youthful; only the folds of skin at his jaw betray his age. A few months later he was appointed to the council of James IV and thereafter divided his time between the royal court and his palace in Old Aberdeen.

Elphinstone's purpose in founding the university was essentially practical. As bishop, he had been made aware of the ignorance and isolation of the clergy in his diocese and of the backwardness of the region as a whole. As a councillor and judge, he had seen the need for more, and better-trained, lawyers to handle the business of the courts and of the state. His answer to these problems lay in higher education, in the provision of a centre of learning for the North. Sited at Old Aberdeen, open to clergy and laymen alike, it would produce the priests, the schoolmasters, the lawyers and the administrators that region and nation required.

*5 William Elphinstone, Bishop of Aberdeen and founder of the university. The portrait, probably painted about 1505 by an artist trained in the Netherlands, would have been hinged to a religious subject, perhaps placed behind the high altar in the chapel.*

First, Elphinstone had to win the support of the king. James IV was still in his early twenties but he already showed the enthusiasm for knowledge and novelty that marked other princely patrons of the Renaissance. A new university was attractive to him on both counts, while the promise of a cadre

5

IACOBVS · 4 · D · G · REX
SCOTORVM ·

6

7

*7 Roderigo Borgia, the formidable Pope Alexander VI (1492-1503).*

8

*8 The city of Rome, from the Latin chronicle of Jacobus Philippus Foresti of Bergamo, printed in Venice in 1492.*

*6 King James IV (1488-1513).*

of well-trained professionals at the service of the crown was an offer he could hardly refuse. It may have been James who encouraged Elphinstone to provide for the teaching of medicine: he dabbled in the science himself. He certainly gave the bishop the backing he needed, and Elphinstone was able to submit the project in the royal name for the approval of the pope.

In an age when higher education was largely under the patronage of the church, papal approval was essential. To win it, Elphinstone had to satisfy His Holiness that a new university was both necessary and viable. He did precisely that in Rome on 6 February 1495, when he presented the proposal to Pope Alexander VI. Alexander was a formidable character, but Elphinstone had prepared a convincing case. He played up the remoteness of the North of Scotland – the inhabitants, he declared, with some exaggeration no doubt, were 'rude, ignorant of letters, almost barbarians'. In addition, he stressed the inaccessibility of other universities. Finally, he was able to show that his project was already assured of financial support. This, together with the royal seal at the foot of the document, was enough to persuade Alexander to give his approval on the spot. Four days later that approval was formalised in the Foundation Bull: the document, with its leaden bull (or seal) is still in the university's keeping. It empowered Elphinstone to establish a university in Old Aberdeen, with the powers and

9

*9 The Foundation Bull. The date is written as 10 February 1494: at that time, however, the Christian year began on 25 March, so by modern reckoning (from January) the year is 1495.*

privileges of the universities of Paris and Bologna, offering courses in the liberal arts and the higher studies of theology, canon and civil law, and medicine.

Ten years passed before the process was complete. Ten crucial years, in which Elphinstone raised the funds necessary to make his university secure at a time when Scotland's two existing universities, at St Andrews and Glasgow, were in financial difficulties.

The bishop drew heavily on his own purse for capital expenditure in the early years. At the same time, however, he steadily amassed lands and revenues in the university's name to cover its recurrent costs, seeking out private contributions towards the salaries of its staff and the maintenance of its students. His efforts were aided by the patronage of the king, who gave, in addition, a personal gift of £12. 6s. annually to pay for a teacher of medicine. Aberdeen thus became the first British university to have what amounted to a chair in the subject, although it had long been taught elsewhere. Lower down the list of benefactors came local men like Robert Blindsell, a leading Aberdeen merchant, who gave 23 shillings

*10 A fifteenth-century lesson, from a manual for parish priests, printed in Cologne around 1492, owned by Bishop Elphinstone.*

10

annually for the upkeep of staff and students, in return for masses for his soul and those of his wife and sons; and landowners like Adam Hepburn who, with his wife, repaid the bishop 'for his many kindnesses to us' with lands to support a student of theology.

In the meantime, Elphinstone had started up a programme of teaching, if only on a modest scale. He recruited teachers of theology and law from the senior clerics of the cathedral and diocese, who in turn attracted students from among the secular clergy and religious orders in the locality. His first teacher of medicine was James Cumming, who was, at the same time, appointed physician to the New Town. To direct the course in liberal arts, he went further afield and chose Hector Boece, a Dundonian, then winning a reputation as a teacher at the University of Paris. Boece drew his first students from among the young boys studying for the priesthood at the cathedral and pupils of the burgh school of New Aberdeen.

11

*11 The Latin inscription beside the west door of the chapel states that the masons began work on 2 April 1500. The choice of day was probably symbolic: 2 April was the day on which Solomon began to build the Temple in Jerusalem.*

To begin with, classes were held in the teachers' own houses, but Elphinstone lost no time in finding a site for a self-contained college. Not that he had far to look. The burgh of Old Aberdeen was already cramped, with little room for expansion. At its head stood the cathedral, the bishop's palace and the Chanonry, where the cathedral clergy lived. In the middle, tradesmen's houses jostled for space on each side of the main street. At its foot ran the Powis Burn and beyond that rose the Spital Hill. A sodden stretch of ground beside the burn, in the south-east corner of the burgh, was the only flat site left for development. By 1498 Elphinstone's workmen began to clear it, sinking massive timber rafts into the waterlogged soil to take the weight of the buildings. Two years later his masons moved in and began work on the chapel.

By 1505 funds had reached an acceptable level, the first students had graduated from the courses in the Old Town and the new buildings were nearly ready. To mark the establishment of the enterprise in its own premises, Elphinstone issued, on 17 September, its Foundation Charter, setting out the constitution of the university and the structure of its college.

The most important office in the university's constitution was that of the chancellor, who regulated the conduct of the university; it was vested automatically in the Bishop of Aberdeen. Next came the rector, elected by the academic community, who deputised for the chancellor and was directed to hold annual visitations (or inspections) of the college. The five faculties – theology, canon and civil law, medicine and the liberal arts – were each distinct from the others: distinct in almost every way, from the length of their courses to their stalls in the chapel. Theology was the most prestigious; arts the largest, with its own official, the dean.

*12 The Foundation Charter of 1505, bearing the seal of William Elphinstone as Bishop of Aberdeen.*

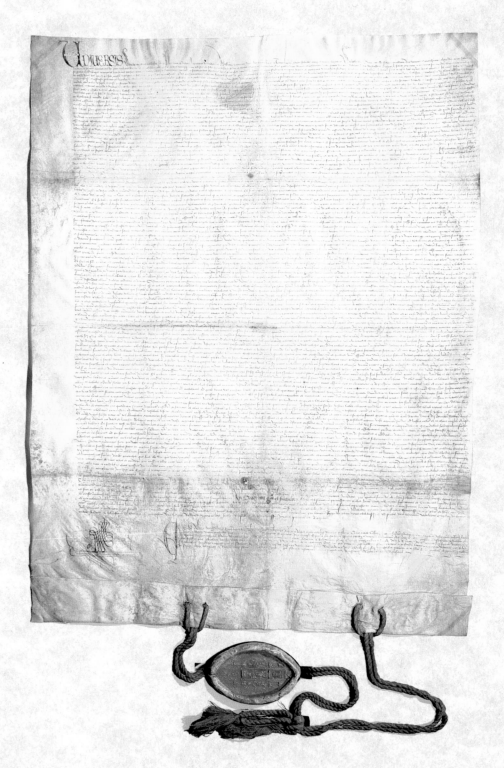

13

*13 The choir stalls in King's College Chapel show a strong Flemish influence but may have been carved by the team of Scottish craftsmen (see opposite page) who had earlier worked on the stalls of the parish church of St Nicholas, Aberdeen.*

The college was dedicated to Saint Mary in the Nativity. At its head, under the charter, was the principal, with a salary of £26. 13s. 4d., free quarters and board and the right to hold other church appointments, provided they were not at the cathedral. These were generous terms, designed to attract a scholar of distinction. The principal was assisted by the subprincipal, who dealt with disciplinary matters, and by the procurator, who handled the accounts; both of them were drawn from the teaching staff. The principal and subprincipal were to live in the college, together with five students of theology and thirteen of arts. The latter were to be boys with academic potential, whose families could not afford to educate them further. They had free accommodation and lived on bursaries of £8 (with one of only £5) furnished from the endowments which Elphinstone had so carefully amassed. Such a small community needed few additional staff. Provisioning and catering were the responsibility of the provisor and, under him, the cook; other tasks, some ceremonial, some domestic, were carried out by the beadle. The chapel was to be served by eight chaplains. They were headed by the cantor, who supervised the music and had charge of the four choristers, and the sacrist, who looked after the vestments and altar vessels, lit the candles, rang the bells and kept the college clean and tidy.

The charter also set out the arrangements for teaching. Theology was to be taught by the principal; laws and medicine, by the canonist, civilist and mediciner. The liberal arts were to be taught by the principal, the subprincipal and a teacher called the grammarian. They could draw for assistance on the students of theology. Each regent (as the teachers in arts came to be known) was to take his students through all four years of the course. The canonist, the civilist and the mediciner would live and teach outside the college, thus avoiding the necessity for themselves and their students to lead a secluded and celibate life within the walls.

In 1505 the walls themselves were all but finished, forming a defensive square against the distractions and dangers of the world. On the north side was the chapel, its tower housing Trinitas, Maria, Michael, Gabriel and Raphael, the five great bells, and their seven smaller siblings. On the east side stood the common school, for lectures, examinations and assemblies; above it was the hall, where staff and students dined and supped together and, after graduations, feasted. To the south were the rooms of the subprincipal and the students; and to the west, fronting on the main street, the principal's quarters. Rising protectively at the south-eastern and south-western corners were two round towers, the first of which housed the library. In the quadrangle enclosed by the buildings was the well; behind the common school were the kitchen, brewhouses and stores; and between the south side and the Powis Burn lay the college garden. Across the main street and beyond the burn were the manses (some not yet completed) for the chaplains and choristers and the teachers who lived out.

14 These scenes from a fifteenth-century university classroom decorate the lecture notes of a Morayshire student, who studied at Louvain in 1467. They show a master reading from the Physics of Aristotle, another delivering a lecture, and a student in a red gown.

15

16

*15 One of two portraits said to be of Hector Boece. Neither is authentic, but both may derive from the same source.*

*16 Desiderius Erasmus (d. 1536), fellow-student of Hector Boece in Paris, later the leading humanist scholar of his time.*

Once the members of the college had settled into their new quarters, teaching began to flourish, especially in the liberal arts. The course itself was conventional enough. Modelled on that of Paris, it was spread over three and a half years. In the first, students were trained in grammar and rhetoric (writing and speaking Latin) and in logic. The remaining years were devoted to the physics, metaphysics and ethics of Aristotle and the commentaries of Christian scholars upon them. First-year classes in grammar apart, the teaching was in Latin. It took the form of daily lectures on the texts, reinforced by questions and exercises, with weekly disputations to sharpen the students' skills in argument. There were two examinations: one in the second year, after which students became bachelors; the other in the fourth year, by an elaborate process of assessment, which led to the master's degree. Candidates were examined orally, answering questions on the texts and debating propositions posed by the examiners. The teaching year lasted from October to April, when it gave way to the examination of candidates for the master's degree; graduation took place in July. There were no vacations: religious feast-days provided the only respite.

What distinguished the course was the strain of humanism which enriched the teaching of Latin language and literature. It was foreshadowed by Elphinstone's own interest in the 'new learning' and by his choice of Hector Boece as a teacher. Boece had more than fulfilled his early promise and was now principal of the college. An elegant stylist, as befitted a friend of Erasmus – 'I send you a few verses,' wrote the Dutchman, 'I hope you won't altogether despise them' – he gave classical studies at Aberdeen the depth, the range and the rigour which were the hallmarks of humanism. Boece's standards were reinforced by John Vaus, one of his first graduates, who had gone on to study at Paris. He returned to Aberdeen as its first grammarian, bringing with him his own method of teaching Latin in Scots and the latest works of the humanist masters of continental Europe, in the new medium of print.

In 1514 Elphinstone drew up a second foundation charter, by which he increased the membership of the college from 36 to 42 and set out, in greater detail than before, the pattern of college life. For students living within the walls the regime was austere. They began their studies early – probably at 6 a.m. – and breaking only for dinner, continued until early in the evening, when they went to supper. They worshipped together regularly: at the beginning and end of the day, before

17

18

meals, and on Sundays and holy days, when they donned white
surplices and proceeded two by two into the chapel for matins,
mass and vespers. Students of arts, as the junior members of the
college, had special tasks to perform: they read from the
scriptures at mealtimes and took turns on duty at the college
gate.

The students were governed by a strict code of discipline. They
were to live together harmoniously, speaking amongst
themselves in Latin or French – but not Scots. They were
forbidden to carry arms, to wander by night as pimps or stray
abroad as 'gallants'. As a precaution, they were locked in the
college from 8 p.m. to 5 a.m. (10 p.m. to 4 a.m. in summer).
Even in the daytime they were not allowed out without
permission, and then only if they were properly dressed in their
black gowns and hoods, round or pointed, depending on their
faculty and status. Those who disobeyed were punished by fines
or beatings; absentees lost their bursaries; repeated offenders
were expelled.

Elphinstone did not live to put his second charter into effect.
The last years of his life had been among the most taxing, as he
tried in vain to dissuade James IV from the rash policies which
led to the king's death at Flodden. In the months that followed,
he had been nominated as archbishop of St Andrews – 'the
crowning dignity', wrote Hector Boece, his biographer. But
before that appointment could be ratified, he died, on 25
October 1514, at the age of 83. 'Bury my body where you
please', he told his friends. 'It was buried', Boece recorded, 'in
his own college, before the chief altar'.

19

*19 The south wall of the chapel, bearing the arms of William Stewart, bishop and chancellor (1532-45), whose new building there housed not only the college books but its treasures (in the jewel house) and its sacred vessels and vestments (in the sacristy).*

Elphinstone's death was followed by four uneasy years, when it was left to Boece to hold the college together. But under the chancellorship of Bishop Gavin Dunbar, the college – 'King's College' as it had come to be called – regained its momentum. Dunbar completed Elphinstone's plans, issuing the charter of 1514, improving the accommodation on the south side and completing the manses. He also erected a monument over the founder's neglected tomb. 'Alas', he said, 'that the dead should so readily be forgotten'. His successor, William Stewart, added a two-storey building containing a new library along the south wall of the chapel. Hector Boece died in 1536, but teaching in the liberal arts continued to flourish under the new principal, William Hay, and the grammarian, Theophilus Stewart: so much so that, when James V visited the college in 1541, he was treated to 'exercises and disputations in all kinds of sciences ... with diverse orations made in Greek, Latin and other languages'. Elphinstone would have been gratified at this and at the fact that graduates of his university were entering not only the church but the legal profession. Nevertheless, King's remained essentially a clerical institution. Although information about sixteenth-century graduates is scanty, there is little to suggest that the founder's hopes of attracting laymen had been fulfilled.

*20 This Latin grammar, by the French rhetorician Guillaume Tardif, was one of several books brought from Paris by John Vaus, the innovative first grammarian of King's. It was later owned by his successor, Theophilus Stewart. Sadly, the illuminated G at the beginning of the text has been cut out.*

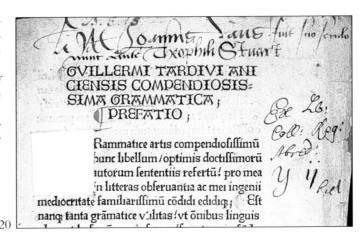

20

In the later 1540s the university slid into decline. All had still been well in 1542 when James Strachan, the rector, carried out a visitation of the college – the first on record – and listed its contents. His inspection began among the treasures of the chapel: 'a silver cross, of weight fifty ounces ... seven psalters on vellum with initial letters written in gold, silver, blue and red'. It ended in the rooms on the south side: seven, named after the planets and constellations, were occupied by staff and senior students; seven, named after the signs of the zodiac, were shared by the students of arts. Their furnishings were austere: the Gemini chamber contained 'a press, a sylit bed [of planks], another bed, a table with trestles, a study with a little table, a little chair, all of fir'. In 1549, however, another rectorial inspection revealed that the staff were neglecting their duties, the students were ignoring the rules, and some buildings needed repair. Bishop William Gordon, the fifth chancellor (1546–77), issued over fifty orders reinforcing the terms of the foundation charters. Senior staff and theology students were reminded of their duty to preach to the public; teachers were told to start their classes promptly – there was to be no occasion for idleness; and students were warned to stick to the prescribed dress, to keep their hair tidy and to shave off their beards. The procurator was to keep better accounts; repairs were to be put in hand at once; and privies were to be provided.

The bishop had good reason for wanting a rapid improvement in standards within the college. The Catholic religion and the system of education associated with it were under threat. Heresy, he wrote in 1547, 'is thriving greatly'. He was probably exaggerating. Even after the Reformation triumphed in Scotland in 1560, support for it in the North East was limited.

*21    From    James    Strachan's inventory, 1542. The Scorpio chamber, probably high up in the south-east tower (now called the Round    Tower,    completed    in 1525), was originally the library. After the books were moved to Bishop Stewart's new building, it served as the armoury.*

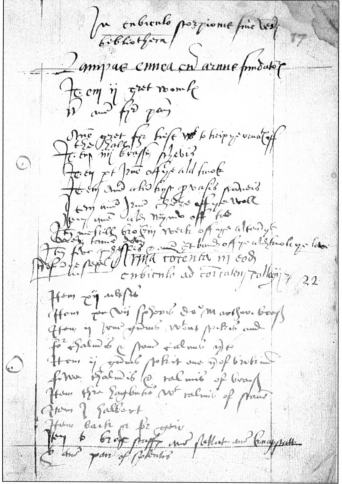

21

Under the influence of the bishop and more particularly of his uncle, the fourth Earl of Huntly, many held to the old religion. They had a champion in Alexander Anderson, subprincipal and later principal of the college. He is said to have organised his students to defend it in 1559 against a Protestant mob from the South and in 1561 fought a battle of a different kind, when he was summoned to Edinburgh to debate Catholic doctrine with John Knox and other Protestant ministers.

In 1562 Huntly's defiance came to an end when he was defeated by a Protestant force and 'fell from his horse stark dead'. The college, however, was left undisturbed, under the protection now of Mary Queen of Scots. But its position was something less than secure: 'At present', wrote a student in

1566, 'some scholars run here, some there, like vagrants in confusion'. It was probably during this time that the treasures of the chapel, which James Strachan had itemised twenty years before, were dispersed, possibly to save them from plunder. In 1567 the Catholic queen was replaced by a Protestant regent, the Earl of Moray, and the church leaders, eager to bring the college into line, persuaded him to act. In 1569 Anderson, his subprincipal and the regents in arts (there were by then three of them) were ordered to Edinburgh to sign the reformed Confession of Faith. When they refused, they were deprived of their posts.

This was the first of four purges in the history of the university. Henceforth, King's would be staunchly Protestant – in its own conservative way. It remained, however, as strongly clerical in character as before, turning out much-needed parish ministers instead of priests.

The first Protestant principal was a young all-rounder, Alexander Arbuthnot – 'a good poet, mathematician, philosopher, theologian, lawyer', remembered a contemporary, 'and in medicine skilful'. To him fell the task of reconstructing learning in the university on the lines laid down by the leaders of the Reformed church. In theology, they wanted a return to the pure religion of the Bible, uncorrupted by the interpretations of Catholic commentators and illuminated by the study of Hebrew; in arts, a new approach to philosophy, free from the obscurities of medieval scholarship and enlightened by the study of Greek. At first, progress was slow, the confusion of the 1560s had left the college in poor shape: and Arbuthnot had responsibilities beyond the walls as the minister of two parishes. Nevertheless, one new branch of study, particularly emphasised by the Reformers, was introduced: Hebrew, taught by the new subprincipal, James Lawson.

The reform movement was revitalised by Andrew Melville, principal at Glasgow and one of the leading scholars of his age. He proposed to change not just the content of university courses but also the way in which they were taught, introducing the ideas of Peter Ramus, the French Huguenot who had developed a new and radical approach to the study of logic and rhetoric. Melville also planned to change the size and shape of the universities, making the best use of their resources to support the new system. In 1575 he discussed his plans with

*22 Mary, Queen of Scots (1542-1587). The letter in which she put the university under her 'special protection... and safe guard' is still in the university's keeping.*

Arbuthnot and they 'agreed in the new reformation of the said colleges of Glasgow and Aberdeen'.

Melville's proposals led to 'new foundations' for Glasgow in 1577 and St Andrews in 1579. Aberdeen was next in line but the progress of reform there soon became entangled in the struggle between Presbyterianism and Episcopacy, between Melville, who had taken on the leadership of the church, and the young James VI. The New Foundation had been drafted by commissioners of the church by 1583 but it failed to win royal or parliamentary approval. Arbuthnot died that year and a further ten passed before the scheme was revived, again without result. In 1597, during the principalship of David Rait, it was raised once more but never formally approved.

Despite these setbacks, some elements of the New Foundation were introduced at King's. It is difficult to say how many and when, because this is one of the most obscure periods in the history of the university and the evidence comes in fragments. But there is enough to show that the ideas of Peter Ramus had percolated into the arts curriculum and that, in terms of structure, the provisions of the New Foundation were firmly in place. The Reformers had planned to slim the university down to two faculties, theology and arts. By the end of the century this had been accomplished: the canonist, civilist and mediciner had all gone, through what would nowadays be called natural wastage, and were not replaced. One thing did not change. Traditionally, the regents took their students through all four years of the arts course. The Reformers, in contrast, favoured the 'professorial' system, in which each regent specialised in the subjects of a single year. But King's rejected this idea.

A key figure in the promotion of the New Foundation at King's around 1583 had been George Keith, fourth Earl Marischal. Ten years later, and a mile and a half down the road, he established a new foundation of his own and at Marischal College in the New Town put into effect systematically the scheme that was evolving only piecemeal at King's.

In the history of higher education in Aberdeen, the Earl Marischal has always come a poor second to Bishop Elphinstone in terms of popular appeal. Even in his portrait he suffers by comparison: sombre where the bishop is splendid, dour where the bishop is devout. Born around 1553, he was raised as a Protestant and completed his education at the

23

*23 George Keith, 4th Earl Marischal, founder of Marischal College. Earlier histories of the university refer to him as the fifth earl, but the ambiguity was resolved during the quatercentenary celebrations of the college in 1993.*

renowned Calvinist academy in Geneva. He succeeded his grandfather as earl in 1581, inheriting so much land (it was said) that he could travel the length of Scotland and sleep every night on one of his own estates. Following the third earl's example, he campaigned vigorously for the Reformed church, calling forth 'such as be suspect of papistry' in the North, 'to give confessions of their faith'. In 1582 he was appointed to the council of James VI and from that position tried in vain to secure royal approval for the New Foundation at King's.

The Earl Marischal's foundation in the New Town of Aberdeen was not, as used to be thought, the last resort of a disappointed Reformer, who believed that King's was beyond redemption. Like Elphinstone's, almost a century before, his institution was eminently practical in purpose – strategic might be a better word. By 1593 the earl was locked in a struggle for supremacy with the sixth Earl of Huntly, who had maintained his family's position at the head of Catholic resistance. Determined to extend his power northwards into the areas under Huntly's control, the Earl Marischal signalled his intention by personally sponsoring a distinctively Protestant college in New Aberdeen, where Huntly's influence had begun to wane. Once established on the lines laid down by Melville and his fellow-reformers, the college would then reinforce the earl's offensive, sending Protestant ministers into the resistant parishes to win hearts and minds and confessions of faith.

Aberdeen itself was eager to cooperate in the venture. It was, after all, the main centre of population and trade in the region, yet Old Aberdeen still retained much of its traditional prestige. A centre of learning in the New Town would help to redress the balance. And there was the purely utilitarian motive: a practical grounding in the liberal arts would clearly benefit the sons of merchants, destined to follow their fathers into expanding markets on the Continent. When the earl endowed his college with the property formerly held by the Black and White Friars (the Dominican and Carmelite Orders) of Aberdeen, the town reciprocated with 'the house, biggings, kirk and yard' of the Grey Friars (Franciscans), off the Broadgate, in which to house it. The arrangement was more complicated than it sounds, and its success owed much to David Cunningham and Peter Blackburn, two of the town's parish ministers. Both were former colleagues of Melville at Glasgow and had been active in promoting the New Foundation at King's. Now they joined enthusiastically in the

24

*24 Peter Blackburn, bishop and chancellor (1600-16).*

*25 The original Foundation Charter of Marischal College had disappeared by 1716. In its place is this 'Foundation Book of the College written with a fair hand'.*

establishment of a new college in their own town and were among the witnesses who put their names to the Earl Marischal's Foundation Charter on 2 April 1593.

But what kind of institution, precisely, was the charter founding? The terms used in it – university (once), college (seven times), academy (fifty-six) – are ambiguous, raising questions about the status of the new foundation. Was it to be one college of a new university? A second college, with King's, in the existing university? Or an independent college, not within a university at all? Ultimately, the authorities at Marischal took the first line; those at King's, the third, although they acknowledged Marischal's right to grant degrees in arts.

Marischal College was designed to be a centre for the study of the liberal arts, with instruction in divinity for all its students. At its head was the chancellor: as at King's, the office would be held by the Bishop of Aberdeen, while the Earl Marischal himself would be known as the patron. Associated with the chancellor were the rector and the dean of faculty, both elected by the academic community; all three were to inspect the college regularly to see that discipline was maintained and doctrine uncorrupted. The college itself was to be ruled by the principal, on a salary of 100 merks – less, commented a contemporary, than that of the subprincipal at King's. Finance and catering were to be the responsiblity of the economist (or steward) and, under him, the cook. The principal and his staff were to reside in the college, together with six bursars. Students who were not bursars could either live in, or sleep and eat out in the town.

Teaching was to be conducted by the principal and three regents on the professorial system – the one rejected by King's. The first year of the curriculum was to begin with six months of Latin, followed by Greek. In the second year, the students were to study Aristotelian logic and, by reading in the best classical authors, were to refine their skills in writing and speaking Latin and Greek. In the third year, they were to have arithmetic, geometry, Aristotle's ethics and politics (in Greek), Cicero's treatise *On duties* (for its moral as well as its literary value) and some natural history, again from Aristotle. In the final year, the principal would take them through physiology and anatomy (more Aristotle), geography, history and astronomy, and on to Hebrew. In addition, he was to lecture on the Scriptures every Monday; and on Sundays, the students of

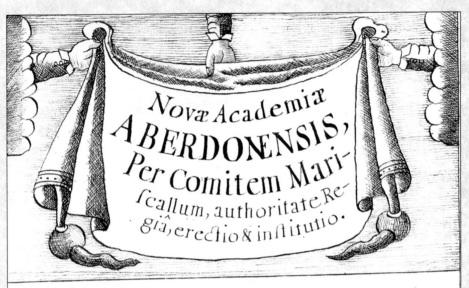

Novæ Academiæ
**ABERDONENSIS,**
Per Comitem Mari-
ſcallum, authoritate Re-
giâ, erectio & inſtitutio.

# eorgius Comes Mariſcallus,

Dominus Keyth et Altrie, Omnibus & Singulis vere Chri-
ſtianis æternam in Domino Salutem. Cum ortûs, con-
ditionis et officij memores inſtituiſſem⁹ pro virili, Eccleſiæ, Patriæ & Reip. prodeſſe, et ſi quâ poſſemus ratione in medium con-
ſulere, animadvertentes, ſeriéq⁊ nobiſcum reputantes, quanta in inſcitia
atq⁊ ignoratione pleriq⁊ verſentur, ut peſſime habeant turpiſſime nequi-
ſiméq⁊ in vita benè beatéq⁊ inſtituenda errantes, adeóq⁊ miſere deſicien-
tes: ut pro innata morum corruptela, omni ſcelere commaculati, graviſſima
jacturâ et naufragio ſæpè pereant, unde Eccleſiæ, Patriæ & Reip. plurimū
damni accedit, quod vel eo maxime contingit, quod honeſta, ingenua, et
Chriſtiana educatio atq⁊ inſtitutio, multis in locis hic vel deficiat vel negli-
gatur, ut piè ac probè educati, atq⁊ in humanitatis artib⁊ inſtituti, quam
pauciſſimi reperiantur, quorum opera atq⁊ ſtudio Eccleſia effloreſcat,
Patria eniteſcat, et Reip. magis magiſq⁊ amplificetur, in Dei gloriam, Ci-
viumq⁊ ſalutem et incolumitatem. Huic nos, malo tandem conſultum cupi-
entes, ut quos Deus Opt. Maxim⁹, ſingulari clementia & bonitate dignat⁹
eſt, cum quod alia in nos contulerit beneficia, tum quod maxime ſince-
riori atq⁊ uberiori ſui cognitione illuſtrarit, et proinde dum in⁹everit
immo noſtro affectum et ſenſum, ut nihil nobis magis ſit in votis, quàm
de Ecclâ, Patria et Rep. quam optimè mereri. Id conſtituim⁹, nō ſine pru-
dentiſſimor⁹ et graviſſorum hominū conſilio et judicio, benè ſubducta

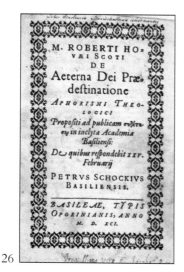

*26 Robert Howie published several of the disputations in which he took part while at the University of Basel. He dedicated this volume (1591) to Andrew Melville, whose ideas he put into practice two years later, as first principal of Marischal.*

each year were to be taught and tested on one book of the New Testament in Greek. Teaching was to be backed by oral and written exercises, and students of all but the first year were to compete with each other in monthly disputations, alternately in Greek and Latin.

Marischal College opened its doors in the autumn of 1593. The first principal was Robert Howie, a young minister in Aberdeen, who had studied at King's and in Switzerland and Germany. He was trained in the methods of Peter Ramus and soon put them into practice. 'I am so burdened with philosophical studies', he complained halfway through his first year's teaching, 'that I cannot give to theology the attention I should like'.

In retrospect, it seems that one of the most significant sentences in the Marischal College charter is buried in the section on new staff. It invited the principal of King's to join in their selection. Intended, perhaps, to make the creation of Marischal acceptable to Principal Rait, it offered a permanent link between the two institutions. Or it could have done. 'The principal of the Old Town', noted an anonymous critic , 'is put on for one of the admitters and yet will not acknowledge this College for school or College'. So began the rivalry and the rancour which were to mark the relationship of the two institutions for the next 250 years.

*27 King's College, around 1640. This anonymous oil painting is the earliest view of the college. The pyramidal roof under the crown had gone by the time James Gordon depicted the chapel tower around 1660. The figures clad in red at the entrance to the college have been taken as evidence that the red toga (gown) had been introduced by this time.*

# 2  Altered states, 1600–1715

THE EARLIEST surviving picture of King's (painted around 1640) shows the college wall and the red gowns of the students clustered at the gate. Wall and gowns had a common purpose: to set the university community apart from the rest of the town. This policy was backed at the highest level: when Charles I visited Scotland in 1633, he was dismayed to hear that the staff and students of King's and Marischal College mingled with the congregations of their respective parish churches. It 'loses much of the honour and dignity of the universities', he complained; he insisted that they should sit by themselves and wear their gowns at all times. So pervasive was the religious and political turmoil of the seventeenth century, however, that the seclusion of the universities was soon violated and neither their honour nor their dignity was spared. At King's, three principals were deposed; at Marischal, one was deposed and two resigned.

King's began the century sluggishly. David Rait, the principal, had served the college for twenty years and was, claimed one of his regents, 'oppressed with age and cares'. Distracted by his duties as minister of Old Aberdeen, he neglected his teaching and mismanaged the resources of the college. Student numbers were low: in the years 1601–10 the average enrolment was 19 and the overall undergraduate population, allowing for those who dropped out from poverty and other causes, no more than 70. Glasgow and Edinburgh did better, while even the rival foundation in the New Town had an annual intake of 22.

The growing popularity of Marischal owed much to Gilbert Gray, its second principal. As a teacher, he encouraged the students to widen their reading in classical literature, which now ranged from the poetry of Homer to the letters of the Younger Pliny; he prescribed Peter Ramus's textbooks on logic, rhetoric, arithmetic and geometry; and he introduced 'modern' histories by German chroniclers. In addition, he laid special emphasis on study skills: the classes revised their morning lectures in small, self-directed groups, received help from their teachers at fixed times, and kept notebooks in which they jotted down felicitous phrases for use in their disputations.

*28 Memorials to Duncan Liddell (1561-1613), erected by his own command in St Nicholas Church, Aberdeen, and on his lands at Pitmedden. His principal memorial is his library, the pride of which is the text of a rare work of Copernicus, written out by Liddell himself.*

Pectoris indicio data frons est quæq profundi
Corde latent, tacitis reddit imago notis
Hoc vultu pietas probitas, constantia, candor
Sinceri referunt archetypos animi.

*29 Patrick Forbes, bishop and chancellor (1618-35). In such esteem was he held, that a memorial volume published after his death contained 8 funeral sermons, 11 consolatory epistles and 40 versified epitaphs.*

After Gray's death, in 1614, his own fourth class declared that 'for the love they carry towards the college (because of the careful education which they have enjoyed therein) they are most desirous to be determined masters in it rather than in any other college within this kingdom'.

Under Gray, Marischal's shaky finances had been improved by better management and there were new benefactions. In 1612-13, for example, Duncan Liddell, an Aberdonian who had made his name and fortune as a mathematician and physician in the universities of northern Germany, bequeathed money for six bursaries and a chair in mathematics, together with his library, rich in scientific works. In 1617 a former student, Patrick Copland, endowed a lectureship (after 1625, a chair) in divinity. In the following year, however, the college hit a bad patch, when Gray's successor, Andrew Aidy, was accused of some unspecified but 'odious miscarriage in matters of his calling'.

Misconduct at Marischal, on top of mismanagement at King's, was too much for Patrick Forbes, Bishop of Aberdeen and chancellor of both universities. Alarmed by the prospect of a revival of Catholicism in the North East, he relied on the colleges for a steady supply of able ministers to combat that threat – something which the behaviour of their principals seemed likely to jeopardise. In 1619 he led a visitation of both institutions, reinforcing his authority as chancellor with a commission from James VI.

At King's, Forbes and his fellow visitors acted on the controversial premise that conditions there should be judged according to the Old Foundation, dating back to Bishop Elphinstone's time, not the New. They began by exposing the extent of Principal Rait's mismanagement and drew up a rescue plan. Forbes reported to the king that Rait must bear responsibility for righting the situation he had created as 'a just punishment of his own bygone prevarications, that both he and others might hereafter walk more circumspectly'. The visitors then reinstated the offices of the Old Foundation which had been suppressed – those of the civilist, the canonist and the mediciner; and they enhanced the status of the grammarian, which had declined. But Forbes was no rigid revisionist: he strengthened the teaching of divinity, formerly the responsibility of the principal, by establishing a chair in the subject in 1620; and he replaced the traditional pattern of regenting with the professorial system.

30

30 *Patrick Dun, the first lay principal of Marischal, was a pupil of Duncan Liddell and edited his* Ars conservandi sanitatem *(1651). This guide to good health advised scholars to sleep well but not too long: at Marischal, they rose at 5 a.m.*

At Marischal, the visitors of 1619 found the gates locked against them. The action was supported, Forbes claimed, by the Earl Marischal, 'taking it somewhat hardly that any besides himself ... should meddle with that business'. Eventually the earl backed down and Principal Aidy was forced to resign. 'I would boldly affirm', Forbes declared, 'that the altered state and face of things hath more than justified his abdication'.

In 1632 the bishop was crippled by a stroke and his reform of the colleges was carried on by his son. John Forbes had been appointed the first professor of divinity at King's and in 1634 became rector, restoring the authority of that office much as his father had re-established the authority of the chancellorship. In a series of rectorial visitations he tightened up administration as well as discipline, regulating affairs not just at King's but at Marischal also. It is not clear in what capacity, precisely, he intervened at Marischal: possibly he and his father had come to regard both colleges as constituting a single university.

When Bishop Forbes died in 1635, he was justly credited with the revitalisation of King's – indeed, with being 'a second founder'. There was a notable revival of learning under scholars such as William Leslie, appointed principal in 1622, John Forbes himself and John Lundie, the grammarian (or humanist). Marischal, too, flourished again: its luminaries included William Forbes – regent, lecturer in divinity, and principal in 1620–21; Patrick Dun, a physician, who succeeded him as principal; and Robert Baron and William Johnston, the first professors, respectively, of divinity and mathematics. Both colleges attracted further bequests: the library at Marischal, for example, was enriched by Thomas Reid, a former regent, later secretary to James VI, while both libraries benefited from the will of his brother Alexander, a physician in London.

Bishop Forbes's own legacy was mixed. A bitter feud broke out at King's between supporters of the Old and New Foundations. It began in 1635 with a dispute over the status of the staff whose offices had been arbitrarily restored in 1619 and whose salaries strained the college's still limited resources. Exacerbated by contradictory responses from King Charles I, its unedifying effects were summed up in the the title of a New Foundation tract, *Philosophy in Tears*.

31 *'Adam naming the animals', from the Aberdeen Bestiary, written in the Midlands of England around 1200. Formerly in the Royal Library, it is the most famous of the books bequeathed by Thomas Reid to Marischal in 1624.*

The feud was overtaken in 1638 by a conflict of a more heroic kind, when a group of Aberdeen divines resisted the National

Covenant. Led by John Forbes, the group comprised Principal
Leslie, Alexander Scroggie and Alexander Ross, ministers of
Aberdeen and successively rectors of King's, with Robert
Baron from Marischal, and James Sibbald, formerly a regent
there, later a minister in the town. All six held the degree of
doctor of divinity from King's (it had been revived in 1619) and
were known as 'the Aberdeen Doctors'. They were moderate
Episcopalians like their late mentor, Bishop Forbes, and
resented the imposition of extreme views by either
Covenanters or king. Their defiance, reported throughout the
country, came to an end in 1639, when the Earl of Montrose
arrived in Aberdeen at the head of a Covenanting army and
enforced the signing of the Covenant. At King's, Leslie, Forbes
and one of the regents, Alexander Scroggie's son, refused to
sign and were eventually removed. At Marischal, events were
less dramatic: Robert Baron had fled and only one staff
member, a Catholic sympathiser, resisted.

The Foundation feud at King's continued to splutter for a while
before burning itself out. Several of the protagonists had left or
were dead, and the new principal, William Guild, succeeded in
reconciling the rest. Changes, nevertheless, were made. The
office of canonist, something of an anachronism, disappeared;
and the professorial system was abandoned in favour of
traditional regenting.

The most important change took place in 1641. Following the
abolition of the office of bishop in the church, the General
Assembly proposed that episcopal revenues should be used to
support the universities. The king, now eager to win the
Covenanters' support, agreed and assigned the revenues of the
bishopric of Aberdeen to King's (two-thirds) and Marischal
(one-third). At the same time, he united the colleges 'in one
university, to be called in all time coming King Charles's
University of Aberdeen'. The events leading to the creation of
the Caroline University (as it was also known) remain obscure;
but, foreshadowed as it had been in the reforms of the Forbeses,
father and son, it could hardly have come as a surprise. King's
had little cause for complaint: it got the better deal financially,
and Principal Guild was soon elected rector of the united
university. At Marischal, however, there were misgivings: the
staff did not join in the election of a new chancellor, the royalist
Marquis of Huntly; nor did they attend Guild's first rectorial
visitation, Principal Dun sending word 'that they were not as
yet resolved with their patrons concerning the union of the

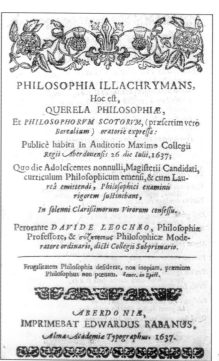

PHILOSOPHIA ILLACHRYMANS,
Hoc eft,
QUERELA PHILOSOPHIÆ,
Et *PHILOSOPHORVM SCOTORVM*, (præfertim verò
*Borealium* ) *oratoriè expreſſa:*

Publicè habita in Auditorio Maximo Collegii
Regii ᴍᴇ*Aberdonenſis* 26 die Iulii,1637;

Quo die Adolefcentes nonnulli,Magifterii Candidati,
curriculum Philofophicum emenſi,& cum Lau-
reâ emittendi, *Philofophici examinis*
*rigorem fuſtinebant,*

In folenni Clariſſimorum Virorum confeſſu.

Perorante *DAVIDE LEOCHÆO*, Philofophiæ
Profeſſore, & σύζητησεως Philofophicæ Mode-
ratore ordinario, dicti Collegii Subprimario.

Frugalitatem Philofophia deſiderat, non inopiam, præmium
Philofophus non pœnam, *Senec. in Epiſt.*

ᴍᴇ*ABERDONIÆ*,
IMPRIMEBAT EDWARDUS RABANUS,
ᴍᴇ*Almæ Academiæ Typographus*. 1637.

32

33

*32 William Guild, principal of King's (1640-51) and benefactor of Marischal, linked gown with town. The son of an Aberdeen armourer, he provided the Trades of Aberdeen with a meeting-house and a bursary fund.*

*33 David Leech, subprincipal of King's, recited his lament 'Philosophy in tears' at the graduation ceremony of 1637. It was later printed by Edward Raban, who established himself as printer to the town and university in 1622.*

*34 James Downie's copy of the 'dictates' of William Johnston, 1633-34. The diagram is from the section on trigonometry.*

colleges and of certain other doubts'. By 'patrons' they meant the Keith family and, possibly, the town council of New Aberdeen.

The pattern of academic life in the colleges was now much the same. The last major difference was removed when, after the union, Marischal went over to the traditional style of regenting. At King's, the academic session began in October, when existing students were examined on the work of the previous year and promoted to their next class; it ended with the graduation of the fourth class in July. The courses themselves began in November. The first class concentrated on Greek, including the New Testament; the second studied logic and rhetoric, and arithmetic; the third continued with logic and moved on to ethics, physics and geometry; the fourth continued with physics, including astronomy 'with some beginnings of geography and insight in globes and maps'. At Marischal, a similar curriculum was supplemented, on the initiative of the town council, with classes in Latin (1620) and Hebrew (1642). During the 1640s an even greater measure of uniformity was contemplated, when the National Assembly tried to impose a national curriculum on all four Scottish

# PRÆLECTIO
## nes Mathematicæ ab eruditissimo viro D. Gulielmo Jonstono in Academia Marischallana recens dictatæ.

Ex libris M<sup>ri</sup> Richardi Irbin

ABERDONIIS.
Scribebat Jacobus Dennans an. 1633

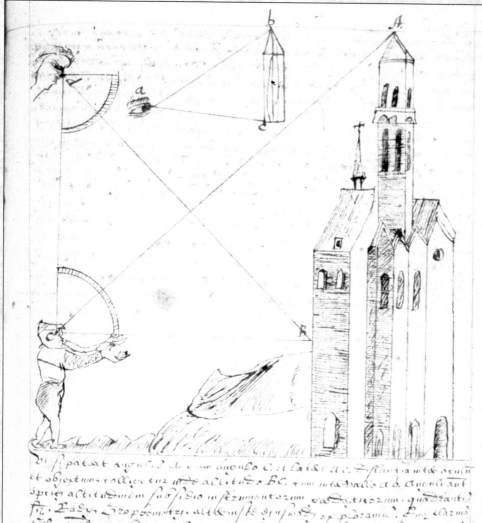

Si patet angulus a cum angulo c et latus a c, distantia inter oculum
et objectum, colligetur inde altitudo BC, cum intervallo a b. Anguli aut
optice altitudinem subsidio instrumentorum radiorumque quadrantis
fit. Radius Prop...metri altitudinis graduum, seq... probamus. Cum duermus
eo radiis patebunt. Sit altitudo turris A b metienda, oculus
mensurantis cum quadrante prospectus in c radius binarios per quod co...
...tur turris c A c B angulus optice a c B b... nef... ero quadrantis depre...
...bus grad. 22 s a b latus trianguli in dacantium. Huius fit trianguli
...te est b... a cuiusnam latus in mensuris vulgaribus pro... fit aliud
latus c B distantia inter a turris radice ulnarum 16. Cum q turres
per pendiculariter exiuntur, angulus a b c aut rectus grad. 90 cui fit
angulo c grad. 22 fiert gradus 112. supra sint itaque ad complementum
180 duorum rectorum gradus 68, qui debentur angulo c a b, quare
fit c b huius anguli opposito c a b partium ma... triginta... 92 ulnar. latet
ab oculis it, huius anguli a c b partium 37 in latere opposito A B

*35 The laws of King's forbade
students to deface the fabric – but
that did not stop John Sandilands
and Robert Udny from carving
their names on the chapel wood-
work.*

universities: the universities prevaricated, and the proposal
came to nothing.

Teaching in logic, ethics and physics was still founded on the
writings of Aristotle, balancing past and contemporary
commentaries on his works and incorporating new
information. Its content is revealed in the notes dictated in
Latin by teachers to their classes. The 'dictates' of William
Johnston at Marischal, taken down in 1633–34 by James
Downie in his final year, comprise 500 pages of text and
diagrams on mathematics, chronology, cosmography (an
account of the earth), hydrography (an account of the seas),
trigonometry, geometry and 'the theories of the planets'. Sets
of notes were frequently passed from one generation of students
to the next: Downie's notes were acquired by Richard Irvine,
who graduated in 1646. The content of the courses also
appears in theses defended by candidates for the degree of
master of arts. Taken together, dictates and theses show the
ambivalence with which advances in knowledge, especially
scientific knowledge, were treated in an educational system still
dominated by theology. The planetary theory of Copernicus
(1543), for example, was barely mentioned in the earliest theses
from King's (1622) which treated astronomy as a lowly
subdivision of geometry; it appeared, together with that of
Tycho Brahe (1589), in the dictates of William Johnston, but
neither theory was endorsed.

Teaching was reinforced by a strict system of discipline,
incorporated in codes of laws issued by successive principals.
Designed to keep young boys of 12 to 14 out of mischief and
to restrain young men of 18 to 20 from sex and violence, the
laws are an uneven mixture of petty restrictions and pious
injunctions. The code of Principal Guild at King's in 1641, for
example, repeated the long-standing provisions against
quarrelling and the carrying of weapons; it stipulated that
teachers and servants should be treated with respect; it
promoted modesty in deportment and civility at table; and it
preserved the fabric of the college from damage, defacement
and dirt. It forbade the students to visit the town without leave,
exhorting them to avoid bad company when they did; it
regulated their conduct on the three afternoons set aside for
supervised sport on the nearby Links; and it dealt in detail with
their leisure, forbidding them to play cards and games of
chance, prohibiting noise and disturbance around bedtime, and
imposing precautions against fire. The bursars, in particular,

*36 An unidentified student, said to be of King's College, portrayed in 1677, wearing a red gown.*

36

were to be models of obedience and humility, wearing a white belt around their black gowns as a token of submission. The red gown worn by the other students may have been introduced around this time, although its origins are uncertain.

At both colleges the enforcement of discipline was the responsibility of the hebdomadar – the regent appointed on a weekly rota to supervise the students. He was assisted by censors – bursars appointed to report fellow-students who played truant, misbehaved in class, swore, or conversed in Scots instead of Latin or Greek. The punishments for such crimes

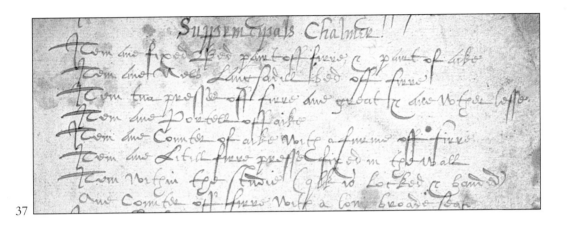

37

were graded by Principal Guild: at the bottom of the scale was 'the prudent remedy of words'; next came 'the severity of the rod', in some cases mitigated by a fine; lastly, for repeated offences, there was a combination of beating and expulsion.

The reiteration of the same laws over the years shows how often discipline broke down, a problem by no means confined to the universities of Aberdeen. Seclusion itself was almost impossible to enforce, when the distractions of town life lay just beyond the walls. Early in the century, for example, a court held by King's jointly with the magistrates of Old Aberdeen forbade townsfolk to lend money to students and banished a couple who had seduced boys from their studies. Within the walls, indiscipline was made worse by overcrowding. The buildings of the colleges were old and dilapidated and, as student numbers gradually rose, pressure on the remaining accommodation increased. At Marischal, the problem was acute: in 1633, 'for scarcity of chambers and want of beds ... sundry scholars were forced to lie in the town house to the great hindrance of their studies', until the town council allowed the college to construct a dormitory. When the Latin class was revived in 1649, pupils were taught in Greyfriars Church, 'since there are not chambers in the college to be spared for them'. Not surprisingly, a growing number of students from both King's and Marischal lodged in the two towns: they were officially subject to college discipline but were, inevitably, harder to control.

The colleges found the upkeep of their ageing buildings a heavy burden. At King's, both the Old Foundation party and the New agreed in 1638 that the fabric was 'like to go to ruin

*38 The seventeenth-century gateway to Marischal, built on land given by William Guild. It was demolished with other buildings in Broad Street, when the college was extended in 1893.*

38

for means to uphold it', and part of the grant of 1641 was to be used for roof repairs. At Marischal, access was improved in 1633, when a gateway was opened on Broadgate; it survived until 1893. In 1639 the eastern quarter of the college was destroyed by fire: the destruction would have been greater but for the prompt action of some sailors, who saw the danger from their ship in the harbour and helped the townsfolk to put out the fire and rescue the library. The damaged portion was rebuilt three years later with funds given by Principal Dun and the town council.

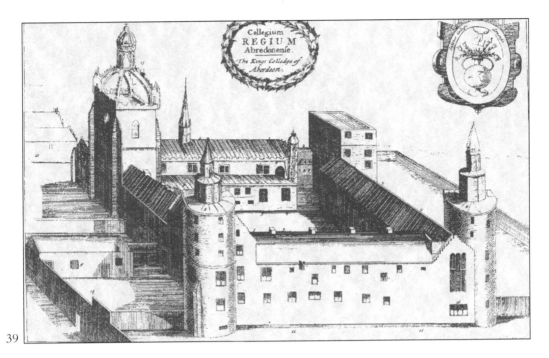

39

The political and religious upheavals of the 1640s left Scotland in disarray and, by 1649, under the control of the zealots of the Kirk. King's suffered its second purge of the century when the General Assembly deposed as 'malignants' (men of royalist leanings) Principal Guild, Subprincipal Alexander Middleton and two regents. The Assembly's representatives could not agree on a new principal, however, and Guild was reinstated. The principalship of Marischal became vacant around the same time on the death of Patrick Dun and passed to the professor of mathematics, William Moir. Three years later, Scotland was under the rule of the Commonwealth, backed by the occupying English army of General Monck, and English commissioners ensured that the universities were governed by men acceptable to the new regime. Principal Guild was ejected again and replaced this time by John Row, formerly a Presbyterian, now an Independent in religion. Principal Moir – 'a rank Independent', claimed a former student – retained his post.

Officially, the university remained united. In 1654 the Lord Protector, Oliver Cromwell, referred to it as 'the University of Aberdeen' and to King's and Marischal as 'the Colleges of Old and New Aberdeen'. Since the execution of the Marquis of Huntly in 1649, however, the university had been without a

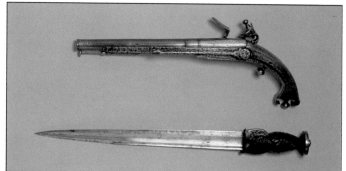

40

chancellor and the rectorship also seems to have been in abeyance. For most of the Interregnum, therefore, Principals Row and Moir ruled autonomously, subject only to the Commissioners for Visiting Universities, whose main concern was now to ensure a supply of religiously correct ministers.

At King's, Principal Row stamped his character on every aspect of college life. A Hebrew scholar – he had given the Hebrew class at Marischal – he assigned himself and his subject a prominent place in the teaching programme. An ex-schoolmaster as well as a divine, he cracked down on indiscipline, issuing an elaborate code of laws, which timetabled the students' day from 5 a.m., when they were roused by the great bell, to 9 p.m., when they retired to their private devotions. He also regulated their work and conduct during the vacation, from July to October. To solve the problem of accommodation, Row revived a plan made in his predecessor's time: in 1658 the sturdy, six-storied block, now called the Cromwell Tower, rose at the north-eastern corner of the college, funded largely by contributions from the staff and from army officers quartered in Aberdeen. It can be seen, nearly completed, in James Gordon's bird's-eye plan (1660).

Less is known of events at Marischal under Principal Moir. The college succeeded in attracting further bursaries, notably from the deposed and disenchanted ex-principal of King's, William Guild. In addition, Moir drew up a rebuilding project in 1659, soliciting funds from Oxford and Cambridge, and Eton College.

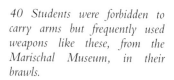

*40 Students were forbidden to carry arms but frequently used weapons like these, from the Marischal Museum, in their brawls.*

During the 1650s relations between King's and Marischal deteriorated, as the colleges competed to recruit students. In the enforced calm of the Interregnum, under a Protector determined to offer the universities 'both countenance and

41

42

*41 James Gregory (1638-75). A Marischal graduate of 1657, he invented the reflecting telescope and was a distinguished mathematician. His son and two grandsons held the chair of medicine at King's for almost forty years.*

*42 Gilbert Burnet (1643-1715). A classfellow of James Gregory, graduating aged 14, he became Bishop of Salisbury, adviser to William and Mary and historian 'of his own time'. He endowed bursaries at Marischal and also bequeathed to the college the sumptuous fifteenth-century Burnet Psalter.*

encouragement ... for the better training up of youth in piety and good literature', numbers rose, giving both colleges undergraduate populations of around 100. They habitually poached each other's students, however, and the situation was made worse when the students themselves migrated from one college to the other. In 1654, for example, Robert Ferguson (later known as Ferguson the Plotter) 'kindled a flame and led twelve students out of the fourth class with him' to Marischal. In 1659 ill-feeling escalated into violence, when a band of armed students from Marischal invaded the Old Town. John Sinclair of Ulbster, one of several King's men lodging with the college porter, was an early victim: 'They did bestow on me many grave blows with iron clubs upon my head ... and did throw me under their foot in the gutter and there again did renew their unmerciful striking of me'. The townsfolk, too, were molested: John's landlady suffered a miscarriage as a result. King's appealed to General Monck himself 'that our seminaries may no longer be theatres of blood', and a settlement was reached. But resentment smouldered on.

Following the Restoration, the union of 1641 was annulled. King's was once again a separate university and, with the restoration of Episcopacy, the Bishop of Aberdeen was again its chancellor. Despite his efforts to win the favour of Charles II with a fulsome poem, John Row became the third principal to be deposed that century. In 1662 the post was filled by Alexander Middleton, the subprincipal ejected in 1649; he held it until 1684. The Foundation Charter of Marischal was confirmed by Parliament and the college remained under the patronage of the Keiths. Principal Moir resigned, however, and was replaced by James Leslie. In 1678 Leslie was arrested for criticising the policies of the Duke of Lauderdale, the king's chief minister in Scotland, and became the first principal of Marischal to be deposed (the second, counting Andrew Aidy's enforced resignation). He was succeeded by Robert Paterson.

The confirmation of Marischal's charter did nothing to clarify the status of the college in relation to King's, and the issue remained a source of discord. In 1669 the Privy Council judged that 'precedency ... does undoubtedly belong to the university', meaning King's; but the problem did not go away. The position was made worse by the continued competition for students, the regents of both colleges 'in time of vacation going through the country and enticing the scholars from the one to the other'. King's seems to have had the more effective

43

*43 Henry Scougal (1650-78). His* Life of God in the soul of man, *published in 1677 at the insistence of Gilbert Burnet, had a wide influence in the eighteenth century.*

recruitment machine: during the 1660s the average annual number of students entering the arts class there soared to 65, while at Marischal it remained under 30. As before, friction flared into violence. In the winter of 1668-69 a series of skirmishes in the New Town and the Old forced the Privy Council to mediate between the colleges. The settlement did not last long, however, and the indiscriminate admission of students caused trouble for the rest of the century.

Academic life at King's in this period is described in the earliest printed history of the two universities (1677). The account begins in September, when 'a problem is affixed on the college gates, inviting young scholars to come and dispute for a burse'. It ends in July, when candidates for the degree of Master of Arts, 'apparelled in black', enter the public school at 10 a.m. and 'the disputes ... continue until four or five of the clock'. Graduation follows and 'is ended with clapping of hands, sounding of trumpets, shouting, etcetera'. Graduation theses of this time from both colleges show the growing influence of the French philosopher and mathematician, Descartes. Theology was characterised by the mystical piety expounded by Henry Scougal, professor at King's; pedantry rather than piety, however, marked the open-air debate held between divinity students from both colleges and the Quakers of Aberdeen in 1675. The teaching of Hebrew at King's, which had lapsed after the departure of John Row, was revived with the foundation of a chair of oriental languages in 1673.

In 1677 James Ogilvie, a future lord chancellor, was a thirteen-year-old student in his second year at Marischal: 'I shall', he assured his mother, 'through God's assistance give pains to my book'. Others were less docile. In 1665, for example, students from King's helped to abduct a bride from the churchyard of St Machar's; in 1667 they caused an affray at a burial in the New Town; and during the 1670s they were involved in nine sexual escapades investigated by the kirk session. James Ogilvie's fellow students at Marischal were no easier to control. Principal Leslie complained frequently of doors, windows and furniture broken during end-of-session horseplay.

Conditions at Marischal were, admittedly, hardly conducive to good order. On taking up office, Leslie had found walls that were 'fallen in by moistness' and rooms which 'did stand waste without students by reason of under water' or 'was so reeky that none stayed in them'. On the instructions of a commission of

*44 Bill for labour on the foundations of the new building at Marischal, 1684. A note at the bottom relates that the masons had been held up by bad weather.*

44

visitation, he reactivated his predecessor's project and rebuilt the Common School. His successor, Principal Paterson, inaugurated a new building programme in 1682 and work continued intermittently as funds were raised, notably from 'our generous and charitable countrymen within the cities of Danzig, Konningsberg and the Kingdom of Poland'.

In contrast to the events of the preceding decades, the Revolution of 1688–89 left King's and Marischal virtually unscathed. In 1690 a Parliamentary commission removed 21 academics from the other Scottish universities, most of them from St Andrews. Aberdeen got off lightly, however, possibly because the visiting sub-commissioners were headed by the Earl Marischal. James Garden, who had inherited Henry Scougal's mantle at King's, alone refused to subscribe to the Confession of Faith or swear allegiance to William and Mary and even he was not removed until 1697. The one immediate change was to the chancellorship of King's: there was no longer a bishop to fill the office and it was left vacant until 1700. Despite their outward conformity to the new order, however, King's and Marischal remained conservative in spirit, still tinged with the mystical piety of the 1670s and sympathetic to Jacobitism. They stayed that way for the next 25 years  but for very different reasons.

During the 1690s King's was, in effect, a closed corporation. There was no chancellor, and for much of the time no rector, to regulate its affairs; the Parliamentary commissioners who visited the college were mainly concerned with teaching and discipline. The staff came almost entirely from two extended families, closely linked to the local landed gentry: Alexander Middleton himself had been succeeded as principal by his son George; and by 1696 George had five relatives around him, four from branches of the Gordon family. The staff controlled, directly or indirectly, most new appointments: only two chairs, those of divinity (filled by the Synod of Aberdeen) and oriental languages (after 1698, filled by the crown), lay outside their influence. For much of the 1690s, this tightly-knit community was united in outlook, but eventually it split along family lines into Jacobites and Whigs, who then fought over each vacancy. The Jacobite faction, however, remained on top, led by the principal and strengthened by the election of the Jacobite Earls of Erroll as chancellors in 1700 and 1705.

Marischal, in contrast, was open to outside influence. Appointments to five of its seven posts were made by the Keiths, who paid lip service to the new regime but were Jacobites and Episcopalians at heart. Their protégés, from Principal Paterson downwards, reflected their views: six were to be involved, one way or another, in the Jacobite rising of 1715. Appointments to the chairs of divinity and mathematics were filled by the town council: it followed the Keiths' lead but was more cautious in its choices. Patronage, rather than kinship, was what counted at Marischal and, unaffected by divisions along family lines, Jacobitism was even stronger than at King's.

Towards the end of the seventeenth century, the structure of the academic year was changed. For many years students had tended to drift away around April as their money ran out or they were needed at home. The colleges had tried to prevent it at first but now they capitulated, bringing graduation forward from July to May (at Marischal in the 1680s; at King's by 1705).

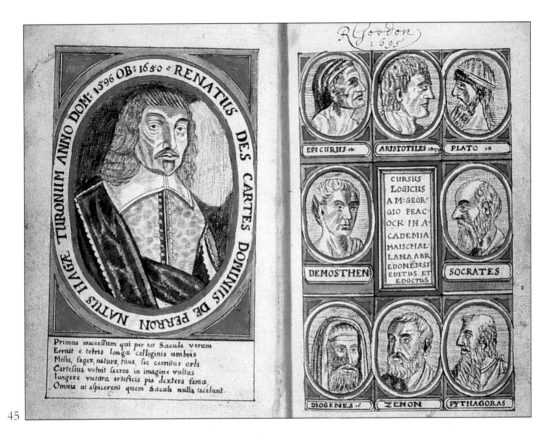

45

*45 Dictates of George Peacock at Marischal (1688-89), in a fair copy decorated with a portrait of Descartes.*

Teaching itself changed little. Both colleges followed the same basic pattern: Greek in the first year, logic in the second, ethics in the third and physics in the fourth; and both retained the traditional regenting system. There was, however, a growing emphasis on uniformity within each college: in 1695 Marischal staff explained that 'we have all agreed upon, and teach the same courses'. There was also a measure of uniformity between the colleges: identical lectures in logic were given around 1700. The principle was taken further when the idea of a national curriculum was revived by the Parliamentary Commission of 1690. Each university was to contribute the 'heads of lectures' and a course outline for a section: King's was assigned 'special' physics; Marischal, 'general' physics. But the plan, as before, came to nothing.

Dictates and theses show the strong influence of Descartes – a set of dictates from 1695 is adorned with his portrait – but they also reveal the gradual assimilation of new ideas. In logic and metaphysics, the theories of John Locke were beginning to win acceptance, though not by every regent. In ethics, the ideas of Thomas Hobbes and the theologian, Henry More, were discussed: alone among the Scottish universities, the courses taught in Aberdeen dealt with the nature of government and society, a trend started by Henry Scougal at King's in the 1670s. In physics, teaching was based primarily on Descartes but referred also to the experiments of Robert Boyle and the theories of Newton. Newton's views were also mentioned, but not endorsed, in the physics courses contributed to the national curriculum. Soon after 1700, however, they prevailed.

Early in the eighteenth century new chairs were established at both colleges. In 1700 parliamentary commissioners took the teaching of Greek away from individual regents and made it the responsibility of a single professor. In the same year the Earl Marischal created a chair of medicine at his college, some three centuries after the establishment of the subject at King's. In 1703, the Earl of Erroll was instrumental in founding a chair of mathematics at King's, a century after the endowment of the chair at Marischal. Both chancellors took care to fill their chairs with protégés of Jacobite persuasion.

The student body remained as volatile at the end of the century as it had been earlier. In 1689 students at Marischal demonstrated their Protestant fervour by burning the pope in effigy; twenty years later, students at King's were circulating a scurrilous 'Description of [their] useless, needless, headless, defective, elective masters'. Discipline remained a major concern of parliamentary commissioners and college staff alike; but what look like attempts to restore the old idea of separation and seclusion were generally more pragmatic in purpose. When the parliamentary commissioners, in 1695, enjoined students at all universities to wear gowns, it was primarily as a means of identification, 'that thereby vaging [idle wandering about] and vice may be discouraged'. When King's, in 1700, tried to enforce residence within the college, it was largely as a means of making money.

46 King's College from the south-east, in 1848, by James Cassie, showing its three distinctive towers, the Crown Tower, the Round Tower and the Cromwell Tower.

# 3 Politics and Enlightenment, 1715–1820

I N THE EIGHTEENTH century both King's College and Marischal achieved considerable academic distinction, while at the same time they suffered great political stresses from outside, were constantly at loggerheads, and underwent (especially at King's) severe internal strife.

In the early part of the century, staff and students were mainly Jacobite, reflecting the political sympathies of northern Scotland. Support for the Jacobite rebellion against King George I in 1715 led to teaching at Marischal College being suspended for two sessions, and to the removal of most staff from King's and all but one teacher from Marischal. This drastic government intervention, together with continued political influence over academic appointments and an eagerness by both colleges to obtain government funding, meant that Aberdeen remained politically quiet for the rest of the century. It lent no support to the Jacobite rebellion of 1745, and it stayed conservative in its outlook during the revolutionary times beginning in the 1780s.

Outside political influences were stronger at Marischal College than at King's, because the Earl Marischal's rights of patronage passed to the crown in 1716 and six of its dozen posts became regius or crown appointments, while three more were subject to the choice of the town council. When Marischal reopened in 1717 all but one of its staff were new: the survivor, Thomas Blackwell the elder, was now appointed principal. Newcomers included the distinguished young mathematician Colin MacLaurin who, though he did not stay long, revitalised the teaching of mathematics and physics at Marischal. Indeed, Marischal may have gained something by the extent of its involvement with national politics, as it certainly did through its day-to-day interactions with the thriving city of New Aberdeen. Although it did not elect a chancellor to replace its vanished patron, the Earl Marischal, who was declared a traitor and exiled for his part in the Fifteen, it soon gained, and long retained as an unofficial patron, the powerful Scottish politician Lord Islay (who became third Duke of Argyll in 1743). In 1761 the college elected Islay's nephew, the Earl of Bute, as its

47

chancellor. Bute may have been one of Britain's least successful prime ministers, but he continued Islay's work as a beneficent patron of Marischal. Both Islay and Bute used their influence to make good academic appointments at Marischal, and Bute gave the college valuable gifts of books and a telescope for the observatory. Less elevated in intention was the man who increasingly dominated Scottish politics from the late 1770s, Henry Dundas, Viscount Melville. This change in external circumstances may help to explain the late eighteenth century decline of Marischal (just as internal strife helps to explain the earlier decline at King's), from that peak of academic distinction which each college had achieved by the mid eighteenth century.

King's College was more inward-looking than Marischal. Its geographical situation in Old Aberdeen, and its stricter emphasis on collegiate life, help to account for this. Old Aberdeen and New Aberdeen remained separate burghs, and in this period active rivals. Old Aberdeen had been a relatively prosperous place in the seventeenth century, and it was to remain the second largest town in Aberdeenshire until the late eighteenth century, but its size and fortunes were being overshadowed by New Aberdeen. In 1790 the population of Old Aberdeen was only 1,713 compared with 20,167 in New Aberdeen, and just as Marischal seems to have gained by its closer connections with national politics than King's, so too did the local urban context favour the younger college. In the 1716 purge at King's six out of ten academics went, and the chancellor resigned. In an episode typical of much that was to follow at King's, the newly-appointed principal, George Chalmers, had to struggle to establish his position against the deposed staff, who for a time denied him access to the college records and to the principal's lodgings: eventually Principal Middleton, Chalmers's predecessor, was forcibly ejected. Thereafter King's replaced its staff in traditional ways, mostly by internal election. But if King's was less subject than Marischal to external political pressures in the matter of appointments, it was much more prone than Marischal to domestic faction-fighting, the factions often being defined by clan-like family loyalties. Members of the college fought with each other, and with the principal, over rights of appointment, bursaries and the like, and were quick to go to the law courts in furtherance of their quarrels. Such disputes flourished partly because for most of the period there was no external authority, in the shape of a chancellor, to arbitrate between the warring academics.

*47 George Keith, the last Earl Marischal, whose support for the Stewart cause cost him and his family their link with Marischal College.*

48

The Sapient Septemviri

49

49 'The Seven Wise Men'. John Kay's caricature of the men who ran King's and opposed its union with Marischal in 1786.

Things did improve slightly when in 1761 King's elected a chancellor. James Ogilvie, Lord Deskford, was a vigorous influence over the affairs of the university, but after his death in 1770 King's was again without a chancellor until 1793. Animosities burgeoned in a small academic community, particularly as it contained some extraordinarily long-serving members, most notably Thomas Gordon, the third of an academic dynasty stretching over four generations, who held office at King's for 65 years until his death in 1797, and who described himself as 'the oldest professor in Europe'; and Roderick McLeod who served at King's for 66 years from 1749 to 1815, for the last fifteen of those years as principal. Another especially long tenure was that of John Chalmers, related to seven other professors, who was appointed to King's in 1742 and held its principalship from 1746 to 1800. Whatever the personal qualities of these and other academics, their long memories and numerous family connections made for domestic discord in the college, as constant quarrels and frequent legal actions during the century demonstrate.

48 John Stewart, 3rd Earl of Bute, a valued patron of Marischal College, of which he was elected chancellor in 1761. The other British prime minister closely connected with the university was George Gordon, 4th Earl of Aberdeen, who was elected chancellor of King's in 1827, and lived to serve one year as chancellor of the united University of Aberdeen, which he had done much to bring into being through his influence over the Royal Commissions on the Scottish Universities.

Simultaneously, the two colleges were challenging each other's status, and pursuing those battles too in the law courts. Several cases went as far as the Court of Session at Edinburgh and some even as far as the House of Lords in London. An example is the dispute over the appointment of James Catanach to the post of civilist at King's College in 1743, when the college split into

50

51

50 Dr James Fraser, Secretary of Chelsea Hospital, whose benefactions did so much to help King's in the early eighteenth century. The college offered to pay for his portrait to be painted but he had it done at his own expense.

51 The piazza and three-storied building closing the south side of King's quadrangle in 1725. It was built thanks to James Fraser's gift of £1,400, and replaced the two-storied building dating from the time of Bishop Dunbar. 'Fraser's lodging' was, in its turn, replaced by new lecture rooms in 1865.

two factions, led by the principal and the subprincipal. One of the arguments against Catanach's appointment was that he held a law degree only from Marischal, which neither taught law nor had the right as a proper university to confer a higher degree of that kind. When in 1745 the House of Lords finally ruled in Catanach's favour, that ruling indirectly confirmed Marischal's university status. Earlier that status had been at issue when King's tried to monopolise the right granted to the Scottish universities in 1709 to receive free copies of books registered at Stationers' Hall. Marischal's victory in this case was hollow since, as the Statistical Account recorded in 1798, 'only one copy being sent to Aberdeen, the right of keeping them has been adjudged to the senior University, though they are declared to be the joint property of both'. Given that both institutions had to fight legal battles to safeguard aspects of their revenues, which depended in part on complex old arrangements concerning church property, it is surprising how much expensive litigation was pursued, by the King's staff against each other, and by both King's and Marischal against the other college.

Bitterness between King's and Marischal was always most marked when proposals to unite the two were canvassed. Schemes for union were brought forward in 1747-49, 1754, 1770-72 and 1786-87, but all foundered. Even if the members of the two colleges were willing to discuss union, the rivalry between Old and New Aberdeen presented an obstacle, when it came to settling where the united university should be located. The buildings of the two institutions were part of the problem.

*52 King's College library has moved several times in its five hundred years history. For a century from 1772 it was in the west end of the chapel, now a memorial to the dead of two World Wars.*

52

King's College in the early eighteenth century was described as 'ruinous', but generous benefactions from a former student, James Fraser, Secretary of Chelsea Hospital, transformed the college. In 1725 Fraser's money enabled King's to rebuild its library, which was attached to the south side of the chapel. That library in turn was taken down in 1772 and the west end of the chapel itself fitted up as a library for the next hundred years. Meanwhile Fraser's gifts, which included money for books, scientific equipment and bursaries as well as buildings, also allowed King's to undertake its most ambitious building project of the century. In place of the two-storied building from the 1530s at the south side of the quadrangle, there was now erected a much grander three-storied building with an arcade or piazza running its length at ground floor level, providing a covered area on the southern side of the quad. There were classrooms on the ground floor and staff and student lodgings above. The eastern side of the quad remained as it had been, with the original great hall flanked at its northern end by the Cromwell Tower, and with the older Round Tower at the southern corner between the Great Hall and Fraser's building. The west side, or front of the college, contained the principal's lodging, and the grammar school. This part of the college was rebuilt in the 1770s and again in the 1820s, the second time with a substantial influx of government money. Thus in the course of the century King's had added to its beautiful old chapel and the rest of its inheritance a very much improved southern and western set of buildings.

Marischal College was not so fortunate. Its buildings had been refurbished at the end of the previous century, and were repaired during the ten years after 1731, but from then on they steadily deteriorated and by mid century the college was described as 'a very ordinary building in bad order ... the stairs are not so much as plastered'. At its best, Marischal College was a very plain affair, so well tucked away behind other buildings in the town that enemies at King's claimed that they could not remember where the other university was, its situation was so obscure. But however unimpressive its buildings, Marischal College was dear to the hearts of the town council of New Aberdeen, and they had no intention of letting their university move to the better site in Old Aberdeen. Such was the plan put forward by the principals of the two colleges in 1749, when they suggested that a united university should be created at King's and the Marischal building should be sold to the government for a barracks. The connection thus made between education and military matters was not accidental. The principals argued that the government needed a stronger university in the north of Scotland in much the same way as it needed military installations 'to eradicate entirely that Spirit of Disloyalty ... and to bring the rising Generation to a due Sense of the inestimable Blessings of our present happy Constitution'. But even this opportunistic attempt to play the patriotic card in the aftermath of the Forty-five was insufficient to convince the government that they needed Marischal as a barracks, far less to persuade the town council of New Aberdeen to let slip their civic prize of Marischal College.

With the failure of this and other attempts at union, the two

53

*53 Old Marischal College is demolished to make way for Archibald Simpson's building (1837).*

*54 A classroom at Marischal from a drawing made about 1830 by Alexander Stewart of Laithers House, Turriff.*

54

Aberdeen colleges were left to go their separate ways, retaining and enhancing their distinctive characteristics. Marischal remained 'the town's College', recruiting its students largely from New Aberdeen and from Aberdeenshire, and keen to emphasise the practical aspects of its reformed curriculum. King's kept its collegiate atmosphere, enhanced by its better buildings and by a mid-century attempt to enforce student residence in college. It drew most of its students from Aberdeenshire and from the Highlands. Towards the end of the century both colleges attracted students from expatriate families in America and the West Indies: four made the 50-day passage from Jamaica to join the Marischal arts class of 1791. Rivalry in recruiting had long been an established pattern of the two Aberdeen colleges. This tradition continued throughout the eighteenth century, and was well exemplified by the career of Roderick McLeod, shown in a cartoon of 1786 wearing Highland dress and proclaiming: 'Annually for 45 years and upwards have I beat up, even to the Ultima Thule have I recruited our University'. Precise figures are not available, but estimates suggest that at King's student numbers were around 100 at the beginning of the century, while Marischal may have had substantially more. At the end of the century King's estimated that the number of students in arts (the bulk of its student population) in any year ranged between 100 and 130; Marischal put its figure at between 120 and 140. St Andrews was comparable in size to Marischal, but Glasgow and Edinburgh were much bigger universities.

Edinburgh and Glasgow were able to attract not only Scots, but also many English and foreign students, whereas the Aberdeen universities, like St Andrews, depended much more on local recruitment. They were also less able than Edinburgh and Glasgow to enrol large numbers of 'ungowned' or 'private' students – students who took, and paid for, not the regular degree course but simply those parts of it that they wished to study. With teachers' incomes derived in part from the fees paid by their students for each class attended, there were obvious attractions in pushing up enrolments. A popular teacher could at least double his salary by the fees he took. Academic salaries at Aberdeen were at the lower end of the range of those paid in Scotland, so fluctuations in student enrolment must have been watched keenly by Aberdeen academics.

Attempts to increase student enrolments in part explain the changes in the arts curriculum at both King's and Marischal in

*Dutchess of Portland Tossing two Main Top Mast*

*55 Students from the West Indies faced an often hazardous voyage. Jonathan Troup, a Marischal graduate, sketched this incident in his journal, when he sailed to Dominica in 1788.*

the eighteenth century. When the century began, both colleges taught a curriculum broadly similar, and little changed in outline from what had been taught the century before, though already in the 1730s Aberdeen had adopted English, rather than Latin, as its teaching language. Then in 1753 and 1754 a new curriculum was introduced at Marischal and sketched out at King's, both colleges probably intending to benefit from the example of St Andrews which had made curriculum changes – albeit less radical ones – in 1747 to stop a decline in its student numbers. While the first-year course, in the revised curriculum at Marischal, continued to be dominated by Latin and Greek, with Sunday lectures on religion, the second year now encompassed natural history, geography and modern history, besides more Greek and mathematics. In the third year came more advanced mathematics and physics; in the fourth year ethics, logic, and 'the philosophy of the human mind and the sciences that depend on it' – which included politics and law, and what we would now call psychology.

Marischal College, especially, developed the scientific part of the new curriculum, including practical demonstrations and experiments. The college had already begun to build up its collection of experimental equipment immediately after it reopened in 1717, partly by launching a public appeal for funds, and it received some munificent gifts in the course of the century, including the medical library of Sir William Forsyth and the books and modern telescope given by Lord Bute. It was

*56 Large equatorial telescope made by Jonathan Sisson about 1770-73, which was redivided and optically refurbished by Jesse Ramsden for the Earl of Bute. Bute presented the telescope to Marischal for the Castlehill Observatory established in 1781 by Patrick Copland.*

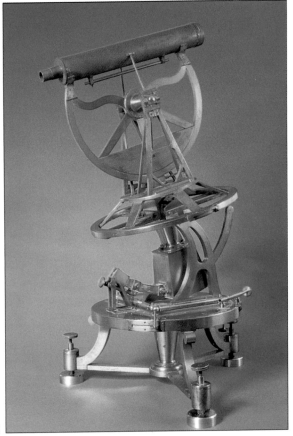

56

at Marischal that Patrick Copland built an observatory in 1781. Marischal also created a botanical garden. An endowment from Barbara Black, widow of Thomas Blackwell the younger, allowed the college to appoint its first professor of chemistry in 1793. All this emphasis on science was designed to 'remove the prejudices some have entertained of a University education as useless' and thus help the drive for student numbers. King's College too resolved in 1754 to construct a museum and a chemical laboratory, but these plans seem not to have been realised. William Ogilvie, who started teaching at King's in 1764, managed over the next thirty years to build up a good demonstration collection of coins, fossils and zoological specimens. He was thwarted by his colleagues, however, in his attempt to start a botanical garden (the land he had earmarked was sold in 1784), and to have more books and journals bought for the library (such expense would be too great, the college meeting resolved in 1785).

57

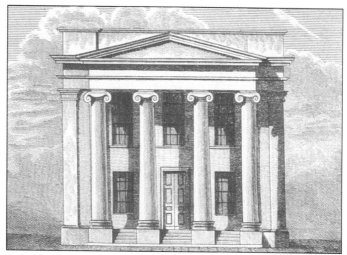

58

*57 William Ogilvie, appointed humanist at King's College 1764. A kinsman of the reforming chancellor, Lord Deskford, Ogilvie promoted the last attempt at a union between King's and Marischal in the eighteenth century.*

*58 The Medical Society's Hall in King Street designed by Archibald Simpson and completed in 1820. The Medico-Chirurgical Society, as it became known, moved to its present site at Foresterhill in 1973.*

The last eighteenth-century attempt at uniting King's and Marischal, that promoted by William Ogilvie in 1785-87, was particularly aimed at improving teaching and enlarging the curriculum at Aberdeen. It offered the possibility of bringing together the resources of the two colleges so that, by economising on teaching which each did separately, they could extend their provision into law and medicine, which neither then taught. Medical teaching was particularly difficult to mount without co-operation between the two colleges. After the collapse of Ogilvie's projected union, the real initiative towards medical teaching came from the students, twelve of whom founded the Aberdeen Medical Society (later the Medico-Chirurgical Society) in 1789. The society arranged discussions and then lectures on medical topics, and these were gradually taken over on a semi-official basis by Marischal College. Marischal had the advantage over King's of proximity to the Aberdeen Infirmary, which had been founded in 1741. From 1818 joint medical teaching by both colleges was attempted for 20 years, but the senate at King's ended that co-operative venture in 1839, declaring that it was 'in-expedient, and even dangerous, to maintain further intercourse with Marischal College' at a time when the union of the colleges was once more under discussion.

Along with the new-style curriculum of the mid eighteenth century came a change in the method of teaching, now finally substituting the fixed or professorial system for regenting. The other Scottish universities had gone over to the professorial method earlier: Edinburgh in 1708, Glasgow in 1727 and St

59

*59 Thomas Reid (1710-96), a portrait by Sir Henry Raeburn.*

Andrews in 1747. Marischal abandoned regenting in 1753, but King's did not do so until 1799, partly because in the middle of the century King's was attempting to re-emphasise its collegiate character, and Thomas Reid - the most famous academic then at King's - argued that the regent was 'a tutor to those who study under him; has the whole direction of their studies, the training of their minds, the oversight of their manners; and it must be detrimental to a student to change his tutor every session'. To modern eyes the professorial method may look the obvious one for a university, but remembering that eighteenth-century undergraduates could be as young as 14, Reid's idea of a liberal education, constantly supervised by one teacher, had advantages.

Another change designed to make the colleges more attractive to students and their parents was the shortening of the academic session, which had happened at Marischal in the previous century and at King's by 1705. Now in the mid eighteenth century King's actually tried to lengthen its teaching session, to run from October to May instead of April, but this led to fierce internal squabbles. Supporters of the longer session wanted to amalgamate the many smaller bursaries, so that bursars could more easily afford the extra month's teaching. It was also proposed to suspend the annual bursary competition in 1754-55 to allow revenues to accumulate. These moves bred further rows and legal wrangles within the college, and in 1760 the whole scheme for a lengthened session was dropped. King's, fearing to lose students to Marischal, reverted to the former academic year.

Habits of student residence were gradually allowed to die out, even at King's where they had been more strongly ingrained than at Marischal, and where Thomas Reid deliberately sought to revive them in the 1750s. A King's College regulation of 1753 laid down 'that for the future all the students shall lodge in rooms within the College and eat at the College Table during the whole session'. There followed some unseemly rows about the fare provided in college, chiefly interesting as showing exactly what the students were offered to eat. In 1753 the second table, where the poorer students sat, got bread and ale or milk for supper, while the first table enjoyed in addition eggs, or pancakes, or ox cheek, or finnan haddock. In 1763 economies were made, with Saturday dinner's roast beef being replaced by boiled beef and broth 'which is better for the students and easier for the Oeconomist' (the college steward).

*60 King's College from the south-east around 1785. This undated painting shows the rear of 'Fraser's lodging'. The pantiled kitchen and steward's quarters survived until 1865.*

But more serious than fusses over food, was the attempt to enforce residence which caused a drop in student numbers at King's, and the plan was abandoned after a decade. By the early nineteenth century there was no common table kept at either of the Aberdeen universities.

As both compulsory residence and communal dining died out, poor students were left to live as cheaply as they could in lodgings, while wealthy students hired rooms and servants and lived in comfort. Some academics offered lodgings in their own houses to students from distant homes, and took fees not just for living expenses but also for extra teaching and supervision. Thomas Gordon at King's had a special advertisement printed in 1744, which stated:

As those who board with Mr Gordon are so immediately under his inspection, he spends several hours a day in instructing them in the knowledge of history, geography, chronology, heraldry, and the principles of architecture: he takes occasion to explain the system of the world, suitable to their weak capacities, and whatever else in learned sciences is both instructing and amusing to younger minds. Nor is their morals and just sentiments of those articles of religion,

# A University Chronology 1495-1995

Foundation
1593

Liddell and Reid
bequests 1613-24

More Aberdeen
Doctors 1638

Saved from fire
1639

Appeal to Baltic
merchants 1682

Closed
1715-17

Reform of
curriculum 1753

King Charles's U
1641

## Marischal College

Archibald
Simpson's building
1837

Medical Society
1789

Joint medical
teaching 1818-39

## Fusion

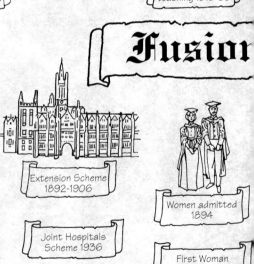

Extension Scheme
1892-1906

Women admitted
1894

Joint Hospitals
Scheme 1936

First Woman
Professor 1964

Quatercentenary
1993

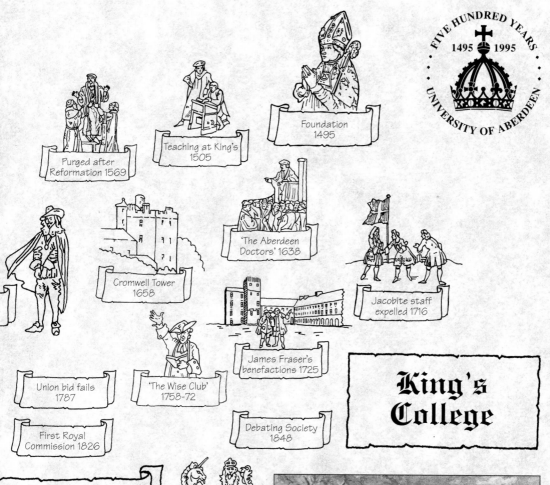

FIVE HUNDRED YEARS · 1495 1995 · UNIVERSITY OF ABERDEEN

Foundation
1495

Teaching at King's
1505

Purged after
Reformation 1569

Cromwell Tower
1658

'The Aberdeen
Doctors' 1638

Jacobite staff
expelled 1716

James Fraser's
benefactions 1725

'The Wise Club'
1758-72

Union bid fails
1787

Debating Society
1848

First Royal
Commission 1826

# King's College

# 1860

King's College
Library 1870

Major curriculum
changes 1890s

'U Company'
1914

Numbers and
courses grow from
1950s

Quincentenary
1995

Elphinstone Hall
1930

Crombie Hall
1960

61

*61 New Aberdeen, 1756, by William Mosman. Mosman held private classes in art for students of King's and Marischal, charging 20s. for six months tuition.*

in which all Christians agree, less attended to, than the school learning.

This programme reminds us of the high value attached in the eighteenth century to 'polite learning' and to the moral upbringing of the young, and it is very much in the fashion of Enlightenment thinking by offering a non-denominational form of Christian instruction. There are many other scattered references to academics taking students under their particular supervision, whether or not the students boarded in the professors' houses. James Beattie at Marischal made himself responsible for the academic, moral and practical welfare of a number of students, though none actually lived in his house. Some students were offered the run of his private library, and coaching in particular subjects, while for others Beattie purchased books. Similarly, Roderick McLeod was nicknamed 'Professor of Economy' by the bright young spark, George Colman, who was sent to study at King's, away from the temptations of London and Oxford, and whose quarterly bills were paid through McLeod. Archdeacon Charles Leslie, of Raphoe in Ireland, commended his two sons to Beattie's superintendence, in part because 'a comparison of the manners of Aberdeen with the profligacy of our Irish university' suggested that Aberdeen was safer for the young.

The disappearance of supervised residence for all but those students who were looked after by particular professors, or

62

*62 King's College, around 1808, by Alexander Naysmith. King's and Old Aberdeen are faithfully depicted, but the observatory tower is probably fanciful.*

who, especially at Marischal, lived at home, may well have contributed to the problems of student discipline which worried the university authorities throughout the century. Early in the century there was a serious political demonstration, when some King's students (like their contemporaries at Oxford) showed themselves to be pro-Jacobite. Despite the fact that the Fifteen had just failed, they persuaded the drummer in Old Aberdeen, who made official announcements publicly, to summon everyone to a bonfire, at which the 'Duke of Brunswick' (King George I) was burned in effigy, and the health of the Pretender drunk. Eight students were sent down for this treasonable frolic, though the university authorities undoubtedly sympathised with their politics. Later in the century the 'siege' of King's, and the affair of Sacrist Downie, speak more of students' boisterous misbehaviour than of politics. The 'siege' occurred in 1770, when a fight between a group of King's students and a party of sailors led to the sailors trying to batter down the gate of King's, behind which the students had taken refuge. In the case of Sacrist Downie, a head porter unpopular with the students as a disciplinarian was, the story goes, subjected to a mock trial and execution, during

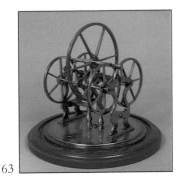

63

*63 Patrick Copland made this elegant model of a low friction bearing used as part of Atwood's machine for demonstrating the accelerative action of gravity.*

*64 'James Beattie and Truth' by Sir Joshua Reynolds. Beattie is shown triumphing over the ungodly philosophers.*

64

which he died of a heart attack. Most of the episodes of student pranks and more serious indiscipline concern King's rather than Marischal, perhaps because the types of students at the two colleges differed. King's recruited more from the gentry and landed classes of a wide northern area, whereas Marischal students were more commonly townsmen's sons, or sons of local gentry, who lived under their families' eyes.

The changes made to the undergraduate curriculum and to the style of student life were not simply pragmatic in purpose; they arose from serious educational concern. This was the age of the Enlightenment, that period when thinkers all over Europe tried to redraw their maps of knowledge, and to adjust their philosophy to accommodate modern science. The ideas of the Enlightenment were especially strongly and early developed in Scotland, and Aberdeen's academics were famed for the 'Common Sense Philosophy' that attempted to reconcile reason and religion. But philosophy, even in its widest sense, was not the only concern of the brightest Aberdeen academics in this period. Thomas Blackwell the younger was a pioneering literary critic and something of an anthropologist, with his *Enquiry into the Life and Writings of Homer* (1735). James Beattie was a poet of considerable standing in his day, as well as one of Britain's best known philosophers. David Fordyce published the *Elements of Moral Philosophy* in 1748 and 1754, a widely influential text which was reincarnated as the article on moral

*65 David Skene's papers reflect the breadth of his interests; they range from medical case-notes to this volume of pressed specimens, bearing the title 'Cryptogamia and Algae'.*

65

philosophy in the first edition of the *Encyclopaedia Britannica* (1771). David Skene was a doctor and biologist with wide-ranging interests, in correspondence with Linnaeus and others. James and John Gregory (who each in turn succeeded their father, also James Gregory, as mediciners at King's) were respected biologists, John Gregory publishing *Elements of the Practice of Physic* (1772) which became a standard medical textbook. James Dunbar published *Essays on the History of Mankind in Rude and Cultivated Ages* (1780). William Ogilvie was a successful land improver who published, anonymously, theories about land value and land nationalisation in 1781. Patrick Copland, besides founding the Aberdeen Observatory,

*66 Essential supplies for a meeting of the Aberdeen Philosophical Society, 10 March 1772. Present were George Campbell, James Beattie, Thomas Gordon (humanist, King's) and William Trail (professor of mathematics, Marischal).*

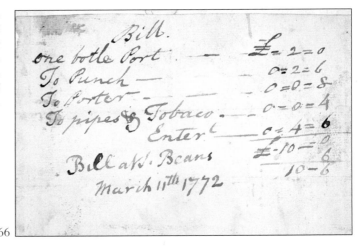

66

was a pioneer of extra-mural teaching, giving popular lectures on physics to the Aberdeen public. George Turnbull, though he was at Aberdeen for only a short time between 1721 and 1727, was an innovative teacher and thinker, whose ideas anticipated those of Francis Hutcheson, the man commonly regarded as the father of the Scottish Enlightenment. Turnbull influenced Gerard and Reid, the men who brought about the Marischal and King's curriculum reforms, which Alexander Gerard set out in *A Plan of Education in the Marischal College and University of Aberdeen with the Reasons for it* (1755).

While hostility between King's and Marischal ran high, and acrimony often prevailed within the ranks at Kings, Aberdeen academics were able to come together and share their ideas at the meetings of the Aberdeen Philosophical Society, or 'Wise Club'. Intellectual clubs and societies were a distinctive feature of the Enlightenment, and Aberdeen's Wise Club was unusual only in that it was more dominated by university men than most. Reading the minutes of the society we find many human touches: 'Dr Skene paid his fine for not having his abstract ready' (11 December 1759) or 'At Principal Campbell's desire, his discourse was delayed to the month of May, in regard he is presently employed in correcting a work for the press' (9 February 1762). Nevertheless, the society's members did indeed deliver discourses and propose questions for discussion, and write up abstracts of their work. Subsequently that work often went out to a wider audience. George Campbell's *Philosophy of Rhetoric* (1776) was a published form of the discourses he had read to the society. Alexander Gerard's *Essay on Taste* (1759) and *Essay on Genius* (1774) had a similar origin.

67

*67 The College of William and Mary at Williamsburgh, Virginia. America's second-oldest university was founded in 1693 by James Blair, an alumnus of Marischal College. William Smith, a King's graduate, was first provost of the Academy at Philadelphia, later to become the University of Pennsylvania.*

James Beattie's *Essay on Truth* (1770) and Thomas Reid's *Inquiry into the Human Mind on the Principles of Common Sense* (1764) were likewise tried out on the society. These were all in their day famous publications. Beattie's *Truth* earned him an honorary degree from the University of Oxford, a yearly pension of £200 from King George III, and a portrait by Sir Joshua Reynolds which shows him triumphing over the anti-Christian philosophers, Hume and Voltaire. Thomas Reid's philosophy was not quite so obviously rewarded in his own day, though it too was famous far beyond Aberdeen.

These were the great figures of the Aberdeen Enlightenment in the mid eighteenth century. Their influence as thinkers and teachers not only reinforced the many connections between Aberdeen and the intellectual life of Europe, but also reached to India and to the Americas. From such heights of achievement and influence King's College had slipped by the later eighteenth century, and Marischal's light was also dimmed by the early nineteenth century.

*68 Marischal College in 1840, by James Giles. The obelisk, a monument to Sir James McGrigor, is now in Duthie Park, Aberdeen.*

# 4 Reconstruction and Fusion, 1820–1906

THE GLORIES of the Enlightenment faded and left Aberdeen in the early nineteenth century with two small, impoverished universities, bitterly hostile to one another and each badly needing new buildings. It is a measure of the achievement of this century that, by the time the united University of Aberdeen celebrated its quatercentenary in 1906, the feuds between King's and Marischal had subsided; the student body had evolved a feeling of corporate solidarity; the government of the university had been totally overhauled; the curriculum had been modernised; and both colleges had been substantially rebuilt. Finances remained barely adequate to meet the needs of the university, but the combination of increased state funding after 1860, private generosity (especially in the rebuilding of Marischal College), and help from the Carnegie Trust for the Universities of Scotland (established in 1901) was enough to meet immediate needs and allow some curriculum development and much rebuilding. The Universities (Scotland) Act of 1858 paved the way for the fusion of King's and Marischal, which took effect on 15 September 1860.

The fusion of 1860 brought a change of mood to Aberdeen. It did not seem a glorious new beginning. Many old animosities remained, and few problems were immediately solved, but at least there was a sense that an overdue reform had been achieved at last. The union of King's and Marischal had been a strong recommendation of the Royal Commission which reported in 1830: now it had come about. Ever since the days of the Caroline University in the seventeenth century the relationship of the two colleges had given rise to endless bad feeling: now all that could be put in the past.

The remarkable transformation wrought, especially between 1860 and 1906, owed much to university reformers both within the university and in the wider world, and to the support of the local community and the former students of the university. Local support could also, of course, exacerbate rivalries. Old and New Aberdeen remained separate burghs until 1891, and their conflicting loyalties added fuel to the

*69 The photograph by George Washington Wilson shows the half-completed extension to Marischal. In the background the Mitchell Tower has already been raised above the Simpson building. The McGrigor obelisk still stands in the quad. The new North Tower has been built, and the old archway removed, but the old Greyfriars church, the shadow of which appears in front of the obelisk, has yet to be demolished and replaced by the Marshall Mackenzie church, integral with the new frontage of Marischal, completed in 1906.*

69

flames of conflict between the two colleges in the period before the fusion of 1860 and even afterwards. But equally important was financial support, as when the town council of New Aberdeen put up £10,000 towards the extension of Marischal College in the 1890s. The Universities (Scotland) Act of 1889 recognised the links between town and gown by making the lord provost and a town council assessor members of the university's governing body, the court. Private generosity was most spectacularly demonstrated when the Mitchell family gave £43,171 towards the rebuilding of Marischal, more than

*70 Charles Mitchell (1820-95). A Marischal alumnus and Newcastle-upon-Tyne shipbuilder. It was the generosity of Mitchell and his son, Charles W Mitchell, which made the recreation of Marischal possible.*

70

matching the £40,000 which the Treasury had contributed.

The main instrument for reform was the series of Royal Commissions appointed to review the Scottish universities. All the Scottish universities were examined together, emphasising how the condition of Scottish education was seen as a matter of national concern. It was the thrust of the reformers' work to remodel the universities in a way that would make them effective in the new conditions of the nineteenth century. This meant organisational change and enlargement of the curriculum, and it also meant that the Scottish universities had to see themselves in relation to the United Kingdom. In the course of the century the ancient English universities of Oxford and Cambridge were reformed, new universities were founded in London and Durham, then in a number of provincial centres. The Irish universities were extended, and a federal

University of Wales created. Scottish graduates needed to be equipped to compete with the products of these other universities, and it was this that led to the changes in curriculum which are sometimes labelled anglicisation: modernisation would be as apt a description. Under Ordinances promulgated by the executive Commissioners appointed after the Act of 1889, for instance, an entrance examination for all students, long discussed, was finally introduced. The MA curriculum was opened up to allow more choice: the old homogeneous arts class fragmented, and more students began to take an Honours degree in place of the Ordinary degree. The BSc began to be taught from 1892.

At the time of the first Commission, which sat from 1826 to 1830, the Scottish universities each exhibited particular problems. For example, at Edinburgh there were disputes between the university and the city authorities, while at Glasgow there were divisions within the academic ranks and evidence of considerable corruption. At Aberdeen it was clear that the affairs of its two universities were being run less than perfectly. Recalling his years at Marischal between 1804 and 1814 the Rev. Donald Sage commented that the buildings were 'in a state of rapid decay'; the MA examinations were a 'mere literary farce' in which students repeated answers which had been dictated to them the week before; while in divinity the teaching imparted 'nothing at all of theology or of the Bible'. Over in Old Aberdeen was what, in the 1830s, the Liberal newspaper, the *Aberdeen Herald,* habitually called the 'corrupt Tory corporation of the Senatus of King's College'. Giving evidence before the 1826 Commissioners Alexander Dauney of King's College cheerfully admitted:

> I have been now incumbent, as Professor of Civil Law, since the year 1793, and I have never been called upon, nor have I given any lectures ... Two years ago, our late worthy Chancellor intimated a requisition to the Senatus, to inquire into the inefficient Professorships ... and to suggest a reformation of them ... I immediately declared my readiness to lecture to the best of my abilities. To be sure, for a man of 79 years of age, it is rather late in life to begin a business of that kind ... I had crowded audiences – no wonder! – the novelty of the thing, and being gratis: the room could scarce contain the audience for two or three nights: they fell off very much after that, perhaps owing to my inefficiency.

71

*71 'Davie' Rennet, the math-ematical coach, who helped many students aspiring to the Indian Service. His contribution to the university was recognised with an honorary LLD in 1885.*

The most interesting point of this anecdote is that a reforming chancellor had actually attempted, though in this case unsuccessfully, to make a professor earn his keep. As in so much nineteenth-century university reform, internal effort and external pressure were both needed to bring about improvements. And there were fruits of reform and improved standards even before the fusion of 1860. For instance, William Walker in his reminiscences points out how strong King's College became in mathematics in the 1850s, sending down to Cambridge three graduates who in 1858, 1860 and 1862 each became Senior Wrangler (the highest position a mathematical graduate could attain at Cambridge). Similarly, Robert Walker, university registrar, reminds us of the success of Marischal medical graduates in the entrance examinations for the Indian Medical Service, where they took first places in both diets of examinations held in 1855.

Before the appointment of the first Royal Commission, the students at Marischal had elected Joseph Hume, the radical MP, as rector, much to the dismay of their professors. Hume's rectorship helped to open up the debate on university reform in Scotland. At Marischal he revived old visitorial powers in 1825 and held a rectorial court to deal with student grievances. Ironically, these grievances included the senate's decision to introduce proper written examinations in place of the farcical oral examination which had been held in Sage's day. Another student and graduate grievance concerned access to the library, a perennial problem not solved until after the opening of the new library at King's in 1870. In 1826 Hume was followed as rector by a famous Marischal graduate of the previous century, Sir James McGrigor, who also held one rectorial court. As a student McGrigor was among those who founded the Medical Society, and in his professional career he had virtually created the Army Medical Corps.

Maintaining the standard of medical teaching was Aberdeen's biggest problem before 1860. With the abandonment of joint teaching in 1839, both colleges were running their own courses, but with inadequate resources. Soon there were fears that Aberdeen (and other Scottish) medical qualifications would not meet the new professional standards being sketched out in England in the debate leading to the passing of the Medical Act and the creation of the Medical Register in 1859. Yet no one was going to pay for two improved medical schools in Aberdeen. Thus one of the most significant effects for

72

72 *Patrick Manson's 'medical schedule', submitted for the degrees of Bachelor of Medicine, Master in Surgery (MB CM) in 1865. He became a Doctor of Medicine (MD) the following year.*

Aberdeen of the Universities (Scotland) Act of 1858 was the creation of a single medical school, situated at Marischal. An early graduate of this new school was Patrick Manson, who later became famous for discovering the connection between mosquitoes and malaria and who, with a Chinese friend, Ho Kai, who was also an Aberdeen graduate, founded a medical college which later became the University of Hong Kong. From 1860 onwards Aberdeen was to provide many doctors for the British Empire; for the army, navy and merchant marine; as well as for the home market. The modernisation of medical teaching after 1860 must be counted one of the major outcomes of the union of the two colleges.

Medicine and law were taught at Marischal after 1860, with arts and divinity at King's. Science classes within the arts curriculum were also taught at Marischal, and when the university launched its new science faculty in 1892, this too was placed at Marischal. One purpose of the fusion was to rationalise teaching by putting the two largest groups of students - those in medicine and those in arts - one in each college. In the disputes preceding the fusion it was particularly the possibility of losing the arts students to King's which New Aberdeen, and Marischal graduates, most resented. A last-

73

73 *Marischal College class certificate from the session 1859-60, signed by James Clerk Maxwell. The student, George Reith, was the father of Lord Reith.*

minute town meeting was held to try and avert this loss. In the name-calling that preceded the legislative solution imposed in 1858, David Thomson, professor of natural philosophy, produced for the King's senate in 1850 a pamphlet questioning the whole right of Marischal College to award degrees; and taunts of 'Broad Street Academy' were levelled at Marischal from King's. When the fusion came about, Thomson remained at Aberdeen, while his opposite number at Marischal left: the man who went was James Clerk Maxwell, later to be recognised as one of Britain's greatest scientists. When the Commissioners appointed Thomson rather than Maxwell to the one chair of physics they were preferring the better established academic and administrator. Thomson was secretary and subprincipal at King's, had taken a leading part in steering the colleges towards fusion rather than a federal union, and had 20 years of professorial life before him. Maxwell, though already the stronger researcher and very well regarded in Aberdeen (he was son-in-law to Principal Dewar too), was still a young man who had taught at Marischal for only four years and played no prominent part in university affairs. The Commissioners chose mature and demonstrated strength rather than the promise of genius, and Maxwell went on to professorships in London and Cambridge.

The first half of the nineteenth century produced few scholars, apart from Clerk Maxwell, to rival those of the Enlightenment. The most distinguished classicist in the North East, James Melvin, is more commonly associated with the Grammar School, where he was rector, than with Marischal, where he taught Latin. Recent research, however, has burnished the reputation of William MacGillivray, professor of civil and natural history at Marischal and collaborator with the natural historian and artist, James Audubon. Foremost among the scholars of Aberdeen after the fusion were two markedly different personalities – Geddes and Bain. Sir William ('Homer') Geddes assisted and succeeded James Melvin at the Grammar School, became professor of Greek at King's and continued in his chair after the fusion before becoming principal in 1885. As formidable in his learning as in his bearing, he was a friend and correspondent of scholars such as the archaeologist Heinrich Schliemann and of Gladstone. Alexander Bain began as a weaver, struggled to acquire an education, entered Marischal as a bursar and eventually became the first professor of logic and rhetoric after the fusion. Later he was twice elected rector, exhibiting in that office the tenacity of

74

75

74 *William MacGillivray's 'Raven' shows that he was a skilled painter of birds, as well as an eminent naturalist.*

75 *This memorial to Principal Geddes by James Pittendrigh MacGillivray was formerly in King's College Library, but is now in the James Mackay Hall of the King's College Conference Centre.*

76 *Alexander Bain and Lord Randolph Churchill in the rectorial contest of 1884, from a contemporary cartoon.*

76

the fox-terrier he was said to resemble. He was founder of the journal *Mind*, and his reputation now rests less on his writings on philosophy, education and English grammar, than on his contribution to the then embryonic science of psychology. Alongside Geddes and Bain were four outstanding medical men. John Struthers (professor of anatomy 1863–89) was a convinced Darwinian whose influence in medical politics reached well beyond Aberdeen as he chaired the Education Committee of the General Medical Council. Alexander Ogston (professor of surgery 1882–1909) introduced antiseptic surgery to the very conservative Aberdeen Infirmary: his identification of stephyloccus in 1880 had been received with 'incredulity and ridicule'. Matthew Hay (professor of medical jurisprudence 1883–1926) served also as Aberdeen's medical officer of health. He inspired the Aberdeen hospitals plan,

77

78

77 *A bajan (first-year student) of King's, 1859-60, said to be Charles Niven, later professor there. The collar of his gown is of cloth, the sleeve cut high on the arm.*

78 *A bajan of Marischal, 1859-60, said to be Alexander Ogston. His gown has a purple velvet collar and long sleeves.*

79 *Alexander Ogston operating: a posed scene photographed by George Washington Wilson, with Ogston's famous carbolic spray well to view. Ogston's connection with military medicine included a trip to see the Sudan campaign of 1884-85, for which he omitted to get leave of absence from the university authorities. Later he served in the South-African War and, when he was in his seventies, on the Salonica and Italian fronts in the First World War.*

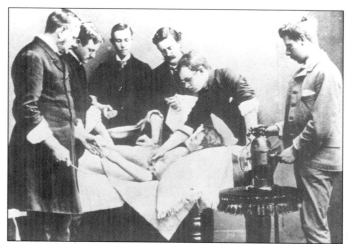

79

which was to move the Infirmary to a greenfield site (Foresterhill) and place it in the context of a maternity hospital, children's hospital and mental hospital, as well as the university medical school. This plan was finally realised just before the Second World War. But of all the nineteenth-century medical men, John Macwilliam (professor of physiology 1886-1928) was 'the best medical scientist working in Aberdeen in this period'. He did significant research on the functioning of the heart, as well as thoroughly modernising his subject. These men and their colleagues ensured that the medical faculty became the fastest-growing and most influential part of the university in the late nineteenth and early twentieth centuries.

A major change brought about by the 1858 Act was in the system of government of the Scottish universities, including Aberdeen. To help public accountability and check the power of professors and senates, two new bodies were created – a university court and a general council of graduates for each university. The court was to become the new governing body of the university, with power to revise the decisions of senate, to hear appeals from senate, and to appoint professors. Senate, in 1858, retained control of property and revenues, subject to the review of court, but after the 1889 Act the court became the property-owning and managing body, and gained substantial further powers. Senate kept only its superintendence of teaching and discipline. At Aberdeen the court comprised the rector (elected by matriculated students), the principal, and four assessors chosen by the chancellor, the rector, the senate and the general council. The 1889 Act enlarged the court by

ABERDEEN UNIVERSITY ARTS CLASS 1894-98

adding two municipal representatives and by increasing to eight the number of assessors appointed by the senate and the general council: four to each body. The idea of public accountability which informed these arrangements emphasises again the perception in Scotland of universities as public institutions erected for the national good, and accountability was deemed necessary because the Scottish universities derived about a third of their regular income from government funds, besides the considerable sums given from time to time in aid of buildings. One financial privilege which Aberdeen had lost in 1836 was that of receiving free copies of books entered at the Stationers' Hall: this copyright privilege had existed since 1709 and parliamentary compensation was meagre: £320 a year, afterwards doubled in 1889. That seems little enough for a valuable right, though it must be admitted that copyright privileges had always been difficult to enforce.

Under the 1858 Act the general council was given the right to appoint the chancellor of the university and to make representations to the senate and court. From 1881 enrolment on the register of the general council was made compulsory for all graduates. From 1868 to 1949 graduates had the privilege of voting for members of parliament. The Scottish universities were allocated two MPs, one to represent Edinburgh and St Andrews and the other Aberdeen and Glasgow. Interestingly, when women joined the ranks of graduates in the 1890s, legal opinion ruled that they could not be parliamentary voters, so they could not exercise that right until other women got the vote in 1918.

Parliamentary and, even more so rectorial elections were often very lively affairs. Every rectorial election from 1860 to 1899 was contested and so were most afterwards. Among the few people elected unopposed were the millionaire philanthropist Andrew Carnegie, elected in 1911; Winston Churchill in 1914; and the locally-based business magnate Lord Cowdray in 1918. Rectorial elections were enlivened by set-piece battles between student supporters who 'fought for the standard' in Marischal Quad, covering each other with flour and peas-meal in the process. A painting by Howard Giles shows the rectorial fight of 1896, while a photograph of 1902 shows weary contestants and a very messy quad at the end of the battle. Rectorial addresses from the newly elected rectors, and also graduation ceremonies, although these were held in King's Chapel before the building of the Mitchell Hall in 1895, were

*80 The Arts Class, 1894-98, showing (second line) Aberdeen's first women graduates; the chancellor (the Duke of Richmond and Gordon) flanked by the rector (the Marquis of Huntly) and the principal (Geddes); and (bottom corners) the sacrists of King's and Marischal.*

81

*81 'Winston', 1900. Winston Churchill was elected rector in 1914 but was not able to visit Aberdeen until after the Second World War, when he received an honorary degree.*

noisy and unruly. Boisterous and even riotous behaviour spread beyond the confines of the university in torchlight processions and meal-throwing fights with local youths. In 1891 'the carriage affair' marked the election of Lord Huntly as rector. After he had been drawn through the streets in his carriage it was smashed to bits by an over-excited mob of students trying to get it away from the police and into Marischal Quad. Old traditions of student unruliness were certainly honoured in Aberdeen.

At King's the number of students studying arts rose steadily from 156 in 1812 (the first year for which there are reliable figures) to settle around 240 in the 1850s. At Marischal it rose more sharply to 237 in 1820 and hovered around that figure during the next two decades. The number of divinity students sharing lectures at both colleges fell from 154 in 1820 to 87 in 1850 – having dropped even lower during the years of the Disruption of the Church around 1843. In contrast, the number of students at the joint medical school rose from 36 in 1820 to 94 in 1830. After the school had been replaced by separate medical faculties, King's had over 40 students a year; Marischal (in the 1850s at least) over 90. The numbers in the two law faculties were negligible. In the years following the fusion the total population of the university averaged 560; it rose steadily to peak at 922 in 1890 then fell away, ending the century at 808. The arts faculty stayed consistently in the 300s but medicine caught it up in the 1870s and eventually overtook it. Divinity continued to decline – it was down to 15 in 1898; law gradually rose to over 30; and the science faculty, opening in 1892 with 12, ended the century at 47.

King's, as one of its professors reminded the Commission of 1826, had always drawn a large proportion of its students from the remoter parts of the North. In the 1850s there were official figures to prove it. A survey of arts students in 1854-55 showed that alongside 17 per cent from Aberdeen, 29 per cent from Aberdeenshire and 15 per cent from Banffshire, 23 per cent came from other northern counties, with 15 per cent from elsewhere. Marischal, in contrast, surveyed its arts students for the years 1827-34 and found that 46 per cent came from Aberdeen and its suburbs and 28 per cent from Aberdeenshire. A survey of arts and medical students in 1851-57 confirmed that around 75 per cent of Marischal's students came from the town and county, this time in roughly equal proportions. A study of the entire student body from the fusion to 1880 shows

*82 Rectorial fights: that of 1896 is from a painting by the local artist, Howard Giles, while the aftermath of the 1902 contest is shown in a contemporary photograph.*

82

some significant changes: 44 per cent now came from the North East, 17 per cent from Aberdeen itself. Of the rest, only 7 per cent came from the Highlands and the North; 14 per cent from England, 8 per cent from elsewhere in Scotland and 7 per cent from overseas. The last three contingents were mostly in the medical faculty.

The registers of King's say very little about the social origins of the students. Those of Marischal record the occupations of students' fathers - translated rather unhelpfully into Latin. In the arts classes of 1820-24 and 1850-54 over a third were from the professional ranks. In 1820 merchants' sons formed the second largest group; but the arts course subsequently lost its appeal for those destined to join the family firm and in 1850 they had been replaced by sons of farmers. After the fusion students in arts continued to come mainly from the professional, farming and merchant classes, in that order, with those from the lower middle and working classes forming a significant minority. Towards the end of the century, however, as secondary education improved, numbers from these two classes increased.

In the 1820s the average age of entrants to the arts class was said to be 14; there was, in fact, criticism of parents who pushed boys forward at a younger age 'perhaps from vanity'. By the 1860s the majority entered at 15 to 16 and by the 1890s this had risen to 17 or 18. It was still common for students to follow only part of the four-year course: 'Many change their views', a Marischal professor told the 1826 Commission; 'and some of them', he added bluntly, 'die off'. As in the past, many dropped out from poverty; others simply studied subjects relevant to their vocation. This practice continued well after the fusion: between 1860 and 1880, 53 per cent of the student population did not graduate.

By the 1820s residence at King's had been all but abandoned: in 1825 a few wealthy students still lived in what was called the college boarding house. Others lodged in or near the Old Town: one recalled 'a little house where there were five or six students, with two in each room and that room so small that I wonder how health was maintained'. There was a steady drift to the New Town, however, and in 1854-55 over half of the arts students had joined those from Marischal who lived and lodged there. By the end of the century, rooms in Rosemount - well-placed for both colleges - were particularly popular.

For Aberdeen students the bursary system remained of great value. Schools in the area competed strenuously in the annual bursary competition. This competitiveness was intensified by the Dick Bequest, an early nineteenth-century endowment which gave extra payments to well qualified parish schoolmasters in Aberdeenshire, Banffshire and Morayshire. Thus even small village schools like those at Kirkmichael and Tomintoul became famous for their successes in the competition. Neil Maclean in his *Life at a Northern University* gives a lightly fictionalised account of the drama surrounding

83

*83 The practical pathology class in 1906. Women students are in the foreground and Professor Hamilton and his assistants at the back of the class.*

the competition. His hero leaves home at 4 a.m. to walk into the city and sit 'the dreaded' competition. He describes the crowd of hopeful candidates, including the small chap with the huge, old-fashioned Latin dictionary strapped to his back like a haversack, and the obligatory Highlander who is trying year after year to win the few pounds needed to undertake a course. Fiction was not far removed from fact, as witness the memoirs of the Rev. Duncan Anderson, who describes virtually the same scenes from his own memory. He travelled down, by coach, from Speyside in 1844 to win twelfth place in the competition. Bursaries ranged in value from about £3 to as much as £30 a year, significant sums at what was reckoned to be one of the cheapest universities in the United Kingdom. When the Royal Commission investigating Oxford University in 1852 bemoaned the expense of an Oxford education, which was estimated at £300 a year for the thriftiest, and £600 for the average, reference was made to the Commission of the 1820s which had shown that at Aberdeen a university education could be had for just £10 or £12 a year.

Students from humble origins in remote districts sometimes suffered severe hardship in order to complete their studies. 'Nothing affords me more pleasure', a King's professor told the 1826 Commission, 'than to see that they have got home with their lives'. Things were not much better at Marischal, where a

84

85

*84 Entrants in the first bursary competition after the fusion included the youthful William Robertson Smith.*

*85 Smith, an eminent biblical scholar and a pioneer in the field of comparative religion, is commemorated by a window in King's Chapel.*

professor spoke of 'the extraordinary exertions that are made ... in earning wages every hour that they are not in the classes of the College in order to pay the expenses of their education' and 'the extraordinary and increased exertions of parents to bring their sons to College'. Proud but impoverished Highlanders, hunched over their books in miserable garrets beside dwindling barrels of meal, are found well into the 1850s: a colony of them is described in *Life at a Northern University*, but by the time the book appeared, in 1874, they were neither as numerous nor as poor as before.

Throughout the century many of the students from the North East and beyond returned there as teachers, doctors, ministers and lawyers. A growing number, however, went south of the border, or followed careers as doctors, soldiers, administrators, missionaries and planters overseas. In the period 1860-1900, 37 per cent of medical graduates, and 25 per cent of MAs served abroad. Aberdonians were to be found everywhere, and in notable concentrations in India and Ceylon, Australasia and South Africa. The university took especial pride in its students' successes in the entrance examinations for the Indian Civil Service. Between 1856 and 1913, 77 students gained entry (only a minority of whom, before 1890, went through the formality of graduating) and years in which no-one got into the ICS were few. The importance of Aberdeen's overseas connections for the hundred years from 1860 quite overshadowed its earlier ties with Europe. Few alumni worked in European countries, and academic links were weaker in this period than in earlier or later times. The imperial emphasis was particularly strong, with a small university contributing disproportionately to the middle-ranking medical, scientific, military, missionary, educational and administrative positions in the Empire.

There were a few Aberdeen-bred proconsuls too, of whom one of the most striking was Sir William Macgregor, son of a Donside farmworker, who took a medical degree at Aberdeen and went on to govern British New Guinea, Lagos, Newfoundland and Queensland. A local boy from Old

*86 One of several novels celebrating 'the ploughboy-student' by the prolific author, Gordon Stables, a graduate of 1862. In it, a Highland student drowns himself when he fails to win a bursary.*

86

Aberdeen, James Scorgie Meston, rose through the ranks of the Indian service to be Lieutenant-Governor of the United Provinces. When he returned home he achieved some prominence in Liberal politics, and, as Lord Meston of Agra, was chancellor of the university from 1928 to 1945. A notable military and imperial career was that of Major-General J R Macdonald, RE, who surveyed the route of the East African railway, was first British Commissioner of the Uganda Protectorate, served in China after the Boxer rebellion, and commanded the military escort for Francis Younghusband's mission to Tibet in 1903-4. Field Marshal Lord Milne rose higher in his military career, commanding the British forces at Salonica in the First World War and later becoming Chief of the Imperial General Staff. One of the commanding figures of the mission-field in nineteenth-century Africa was Robert Laws, who had supported himself through his arts course at Aberdeen by working as a cabinet maker. He planned to top a new school building at the Livingstonia mission station in Nyasaland with a crown tower like that of King's College.

87

88

*87 Illuminated address presented to Sir John Anderson on his appointment as Governor of Ceylon in 1916. Aberdeen has a particularly strong connection with Ceylon, dating from the tea-planting days of the nineteenth century.*

*88 Choral singing was a strong Aberdeen tradition and students adopted 'Gaudeamus' as their signature tune. Charles Sanford Terry, the great Bach scholar, was appointed lecturer in history in 1898. He revived the Choral and Orchestral Society, and succeeded in 1905 in a six-year campaign to have women admitted to it.*

Another churchman of humble origins was Bishop John Strachan, son of a quarryman. Strachan obtained a charter in 1827 for an Anglican University in Toronto, to be called King's College, after his *alma mater*. When his college was taken over by the colonial government as the secular University of Toronto, Strachan obtained a new charter for an Anglican Trinity College, Toronto.

In an international graduate market-place, sons of the rural manse, the parish school and the farm or croft competed with the sophisticated products of English public schools and Oxbridge. The development of extra-curricular, college-based activities, largely on the students' own initiative, helped to reduce the social and cultural gap. At King's the Debating Society was founded - not inappropriately - in the Year of Revolutions, 1848; the Celtic Society in 1854. Both survived the fusion, the former becoming the senior university society. There are no records of societies at Marischal but the divinity students of both colleges formed religious associations. After the fusion came the Medical Society (1865), Literary Society (1871) and Choral Society (1875). Following the example of

89

Edinburgh, Aberdeen founded a Students' Representative Council in 1884. Student magazines appeared from time to time, rarely lasting for more than a few numbers. But *Alma Mater*, founded in 1883 to carry a mixture of news, views, gossip and literature, ran until the 1960s. It is one of the earliest student magazines with a continuous history.

The cap, ball and rifle featured in *Alma Mater's* masthead represented its readers' outdoor activities. What had happened to the 'play days' at King's and Marischal is not yet clear, but by 1850 college sport was organised through clubs - shinty at King's, for example, cricket at Marischal. As team games and physical fitness became important features of education during the second half of the century, college, faculty and scratch teams were gradually replaced by university clubs, beginning with rugby football (1872), and by the Athletic Association, formed to administer the playing-field behind King's, bought in 1890. Closely related to sport was military Volunteering. A student unit was formed in 1885, a separate medical unit in 1888.

Social and cultural societies, campus journalism, team games and summer camps all reinforced the bonding inherent in a four-year course in arts and (later) a five-year course in medicine; and for some students, at least, there was a strong sense of community. What could be called the *alma mater* cult was personified in men like P J Anderson (student, assistant, librarian and historian of the university), J M Bulloch (student, journalist, benefactor and historian) and W K Leask (student, assistant and writer on university subjects); and it was

90                                                                                              91

*90 'Salve toga rubra' (1893).
After 1860 the gown combined
the sleeves of King's and the collar
of Marischal. The student wearing it is said to have been P J
Anderson, historian and librarian
of the university.*

*91 The Gateway, King's College,
a photograph by G A Clarke. It
was published in* Alma Mater *in
1916, but the students are not
named.*

celebrated in the pages of American-style arts and medical *Class Records*. In 'Salve toga rubra', by Sir George Reid (1893) it acquired an icon: the student's red gown is derived from the traditional version, but his trencher, or mortar-board, is an innovation from around 1870.

In the 1890s women were admitted to the university. The issue had been raised in the senate in the 1870s but was eventually bogged down in senatorial politics. In 1877 the Aberdeen Ladies' Educational Association was founded to provide extra-mural, professorial lecture courses for women, like those in other university towns. Its results showed that women could reach the standards of male university students but, offering no formal qualification, it lost support and was wound up in 1886. In 1882 the university introduced a Higher Certificate for Women. Lacking a title to dignify its holders, however, it suffered by comparison with the diploma and title offered by St Andrews and attracted few candidates.

The admission of women brought no-one to the barricades. Several professors - John Struthers (anatomy), William Milligan

92

*92 John Struthers (1823-99), the powerful professor of anatomy and medical educationalist.*

*93 The sixth form at Fordyce Public School, 1898: the small rural school from which Johanna Forbes came to university (she is second from the right in the first row).*

93

(biblical criticism) and Alexander Bain (logic) – were sympathetic from the start, on grounds of natural justice rather than any feminist principles. Later advocates included William Minto, Bain's successor, and Principal William Pirie: 'If a woman thinks', said Pirie, 'that she may attend [medical] classes without her delicacy being in any degree tainted, let her attend them by all means'. Their opponents, mainly from the older generation, limited themselves to ridicule and innuendo. By the end of the 1880s it was clear that admission was inevitable: the question was merely of ways and means. Scottish universities were empowered to admit women as students or staff by a clause of the Act of 1889, which came into effect in 1892. Prompted by P J Anderson, as rector's assessor on the court, Aberdeen responded, albeit slowly. Eleven women entered the arts faculty that year – but as private students. In 1894, however, twenty matriculated in the arts faculty and one in medicine. In 1898 the first four women graduated in arts and in the following year women constituted a quarter of the faculty. The first woman member of the academic staff was Johanna Forbes, appointed Latin assistant in 1903.

To begin with, women students were received by the men with a mixture of restraint, curiosity and uncertainty, masked – as their titles suggest – by facetiousness. The traditional year-names for Aberdeen students were bajans, semis, tertians and magistrands, with first-year medical students called lambs. Women students were named bajanellas, semilinas, tertianas and lambellas. Gradually, however, they established themselves. In 1895 they adopted gowns and trenchers; in 1897, excluded from the Debating Society, they founded their own; and in 1898 they demonstrated their preference for living independently in lodgings by ignoring the residence provided

94

*ON THIN ICE*

*94 'On thin ice'. This cartoon, from* Alma Mater *of 1895-96, reflects the novelty of women students, and perhaps the precariousness of their acceptance in a male-dominated society.*

for them at Castleton House in the Chanonry. It was not until the early 1900s that their presence provoked a backlash. Ironically, while P J Anderson had helped to bring about their admission, it was W K Leask, in so much else his counterpart, who was to prove their most virulent critic.

Rising populations at King's and Marischal in the first half of the nineteenth century placed increased pressure on their aging and often dilapidated fabric. Not surprisingly, competition for public funds to extend or replace buildings fuelled the acrimony between the colleges in the years leading up to the fusion. King's acquired a new west front in the 1820s, incorporating an elegant, galleried museum; new, mullioned windows adorned the great hall; and the Cromwell Tower was remodelled. In the 1830s it was Marischal's turn. The old buildings were demolished and replaced by Archibald Simpson's neo-Tudor design. It broke with the traditional quadrangular plan and incorporated sixteen classrooms, a hall, a library, a museum and rooms for scientific apparatus. A generous contribution from the Treasury aroused envy at King's and the staff there, with the exception of the principal, refused to attend the laying of the Marischal foundation-stone in 1837. The new college was completed in 1844. Attention now reverted to King's, where schemes were prepared to increase teaching space. In 1860 the south block, with its cloistered piazza, was replaced by a row of lecture-rooms. The hall, which had stood since the erection of the college, was demolished; on its site arose a new library in 1870. In the 1890s the emphasis was once more on Marischal. The decision to add the new faculty of science to those of medicine and law which were already there highlighted the shortage of space. An Extension Scheme was inaugurated in 1892, with designs by Alexander Marshall Mackenzie. It culminated in the raising of Simpson's tower (now the Mitchell Tower) and the creation of the Mitchell Hall - their names commemorating the munificent benefaction of Charles Mitchell and his son. The scheme also gave the college a grandiose frontage on Broad Street - at the cost, it must be said, of the destruction of old Greyfriars Church.

Strictly, the quatercentenary of Aberdeen University should have been celebrated in 1895, four hundred years after the foundation of King's College. The celebration was put off until 1906, when the king and queen paid Aberdeen a state visit, and opened the impressive new Marischal College building.

95

96

*95 The quatercentenary celebrations in 1906 were a magnificent occasion for the city and the university. This programme is one of the many souvenirs of the day.*

*96 Lord Strathcona's banquet, anatomised in* The Sphere.

This splendid occasion for the city and the university may still be glimpsed on a contemporary newsreel. This does not, unfortunately, show the great feast which Lord Strathcona provided. Donald Alexander Smith, 1st Baron Strathcona, came from Archiestown, near Elgin. He entered the Hudson's Bay Company as a boy, and ended as its governor. He was a popular rector in 1899-1902, one of the very few of that period to be elected unopposed. He served as chancellor of the university from 1903 to 1914. The Strathcona banquet by its lavishness, attracted almost as much attention as the more solemn ceremonies.

*97 Marischal College as completed in 1906. A photograph from the George Washington Wilson studio. The glistening facade rises above the huddle of older buildings which still fronted Marischal from across Broad Street.*

# 5 From Quatercenary to Quincentenary, 1906-1995

*98 Kilted buglers of U Company, Gordon Highlanders, from the memorial window in King's College Chapel, designed by Douglas Strachan, commemorating the university's dead of the First World War.*

AFTER THE CELEBRATIONS of 1906, the years leading up to the quincentenary in 1995 were seldom easy for Aberdeen University. Much was achieved, but in often difficult circumstances and with the kind of personal resilience the early members of the university had shown when they had to cope with the collapse of their Crown Tower in 1633. The character of the university was tested by financial stringency, especially in the interwar period and after 1981. More than most British universities, Aberdeen had to maintain a difficult balance between its regional responsibilities and its national and international role. It had also, of course, to survive two World Wars.

The First World War hit Aberdeen hard. Volunteer soldiering had been popular among students, but Aberdeen had no Officer Training Corps. Instead, its students formed U Company in the Territorial Army Reserve of the local regiment, the Gordon Highlanders. Medical students joined a unit attached to the 1st Highland Field Ambulance, Royal Army Medical Corps. When war broke out in 1914 the territorials were attending their annual camp, and thus a hundred students went as a body to war. Within a year half the young men who had marched away with U Company were dead. By the war's end, the roll of honour included 341 dead, out of the 2,852 men and women who served. Already, before the end of the war, there was an annual chapel service at which the names of the fallen were read out, and the post-war tradition of University Remembrance Day services continues in Aberdeen to the present. During the war Principal Adam Smith proudly wore the uniform of an army chaplain, and was proud too that his pre-war publication of a geography of the Bible lands was of practical use to the British army fighting in Mesopotamia. But his reading of the casualty lists in the chapel was a harrowing personal experience for one who himself lost two sons in the war.

The casualties of the Second World War were nothing like so large as those of the First, but again the university supported the war effort fully and vigorously. Staff and students joined the

99 Three scenes depicting war and peace from the eight mural panels in the Student Union, painted by Robert Sivell with Alberto Morocco and Gordon S Cameron. The murals cover 1,300 square feet and were painted between 1939 and 1953. They have been described as: 'the greatest mural painting carried out in Scotland during this century'.

100

*100 Mary Esslemont (1891-1984), in the robes of SRC president. She had graduated BSc in 1914 and MA in 1915 before beginning to study medicine. She was thus a mature student when elected president in 1922.*

armed forces, while those left behind carried out war work including fire watching and air-raid warden duties. Short courses were put on to train radar operators and airmen. A stack of bombs fell on the playing fields at King's, and shook but did not seriously damage its buildings. The Sivell murals in the Students' Union preserve an impression of the wartime years, with lighthearted scenes of student life giving way to sombre destruction.

For the university, the social effects of war were more noticeable in the case of the First than of the Second War. The removal of so many men to active service in 1914 allowed women students to consolidate their position. In the medical faculty, for instance, there had never been more than 20 women students until 1913, when their number rose to 31, but by 1917 there were 124 medical women, 36 per cent of the faculty. Between 1916 and 1918 women outnumbered men in the university as a whole. Women sustained the full range of student activities, in addition to fund-raising and sewing for the war effort, collecting the moss used for dressing wounds, and running a canteen for troops at the railway station. The student magazine, *Alma Mater*, which had once taken a virulently anti-feminist position, now had Isabella Smith as editor (1917-8) and Nan Shepherd as a contributor. In June 1918 the new Women's Dramatic Society produced *A Midsummer Night's Dream* with an all-female cast. In 1922, the Student Representative Council elected its first woman president, Mary Esslemont. Though she later claimed to have experienced little personal animosity, her election meeting was stormy, and ended with two men requiring that 'Their dissent to the election of a Woman as President be recorded in the Minutes'. It was 67 years before another woman, Sylvia Taylor, was elected president.

In the university, as in society at large, the wartime gains in status made by women were partly reversed in the post-war world. After both wars ex-servicemen came to fill up the classrooms and to dominate student life. There was, however, a difference in the atmosphere of the two post-war university worlds. In the aftermath of 1918 the university became a rather 'hearty' institution, and was once more masculine in atmosphere, though not anti-feminist in the sense so publicly expressed before 1914. This reactionary swing in mood was not nearly so marked after 1945. What students and staff remember of the post-1945 university is the zest for life and learning in

*101 Programmes from student shows, 1936 and 1948, in which Ruritanian whimsy is replaced by a more challenging tone – 'You may think this world is cosy, But it's not!'*

*102 Fun combines with hard work in the annual Charities Campaign, which usually raises more money than comparable efforts in other universities.*

101

102

the mixed classes of youngsters and wartime veterans, and the inspiring teaching and good social contacts with students made especially by some of the young staff of that time. In the interwar years the student community ended the centuries-long tradition of making a nuisance of itself to the local public. In place of the rectorial riots of the nineteenth century came the annual charities campaign, started in 1920. Held in April, Gala Week raised money for local good causes by organised house-to-house and street collections, concerts, dances, stunts, a rag magazine and a student show. Charities Week culminated in the 'Torcher' a great torchlight procession through the streets of Aberdeen accompanied by students in fancy dress with collecting tins. Most of the student shows were musicals, the tradition beginning in 1922 with *Stella the Bajanella* written by Eric Linklater. Aberdeen's journalistic tradition was reinforced

103

*103 Professor Phyllida Parsloe, now of the University of Bristol, is one of Aberdeen's only five women professors appointed to date.*

*104 The other four women professors, photographed in the King's College Conference Centre in 1994, are, left to right, Alison Saunders, Elizabeth Fraser, Elizabeth Russell, Celia Britton. Elizabeth Fraser, professor of psychology, was the first woman appointed to a chair in Aberdeen, and the first woman to be dean of a faculty. Elizabeth Russell, professor of public health, is the university's first woman medical professor. Professor Celia Britton and Professor Alison Saunders are the first two women professors in one department - French.*

104

when the student newspaper *Gaudie* was launched in 1934.

For the staff, wartime changes were less marked than for students. In both wars staff members served their country with distinction, but those who returned did not return to remarkably different university worlds. Women staff progressed less than might have been expected as a result of either war. During the First World War some attained academic positions which they might not otherwise have reached, but even at the beginning of the Second World War only one woman was a university lecturer in her own right, and wartime gains were lost after 1945. The highest proportion of women on the full-time academic staff was seen in 1945 (16 per cent). Thereafter the number of women staff grew more slowly than the expansion of total staff numbers, so that by 1980 the proportion of women staff (9 per cent) was half what it had been at the end of the war, and Aberdeen lagged behind British universities as a whole in its appointment of women. Aberdeen was remarkably chary too of appointing women professors. At the time of writing the university has had only five women professors in its nearly five hundred years of history; and did not make its first female professorial appointment until 1964.

105

106

*105 A soil science student gets to the root of a problem.*

*106 New students arriving at Aberdeen are met at the station by SRC members, whose red togas make them easily identifiable.*

The explanation for Aberdeen's relative conservatism may lie, in part, in the character of an area which felt remote from metropolitan trends, and which depended on a predominately rural economy - until the discovery of North Sea oil in the 1960s. The university itself was, until the 1950s, a small institution, which grew rather erratically. The undergraduate total just passed the thousand mark in 1909, but during the First World War, again in the 1920s and 1930s, and once more during the Second World War, numbers fell, so that by 1945 there were only 271 more students than there had been in 1909. Then came rapid bursts of growth in the immediate postwar years, in the early parts of the 1950s, 1960s and 1970s, and steadier growth through the 1980s, such that by 1994 a university of ten thousand students was achieved. In the large university of the last two decades, four changes within the student population are notable. Women students have come almost to equal men in number, having never been more than 39 per cent of the student population before the Second World War. Postgraduate numbers have increased out of recognition: there were only 27 postgraduate students in 1945 but 1,625 in 1994. Mainly among postgraduates, but also within the undergraduate population, overseas student numbers have expanded, from 3 per cent in 1945 to 7 per cent of the much bigger university today. Overseas postgraduates come from about eighty different countries but undergraduates are mainly young Americans doing a year abroad, and young Europeans studying in Aberdeen on one of the many exchange schemes that have marked the growing bonds between member states of the European Community. The fourth change within the

*107 The university's Lighthouse Field Station on the Moray Firth is the base for the study of dolphins.*

107

student population has been the increase in the number of mature undergraduates, defined in the 1980s as those aged 21 or older at their time of entry. Mature students are no innovation in a university which took many such in the nineteenth century, and saw two generations of wartime veterans through its classrooms in this century, but the larger proportion of mature students, reaching a quarter of the undergraduate population by the end of the 1980s is indeed striking. Aberdeen was traditionally more friendly to mature students, and to those with non-standard entry qualifications, than were many British universities.

Thus the expansion of the university in this century was concentrated in the period after 1950, and was not steady then. In outline Aberdeen's experience did not differ greatly from that of the British system as a whole, but the swings up and down of student numbers were more violent here than in most other places, requiring great skill and dedication from the staff - whether they were striving to teach larger numbers or to manage on less money. The pattern of growth and retrenchment had major financial consequences, because Aberdeen, like all other British universities, depended throughout this century on government grants. Low numbers in the interwar period meant very real financial constraints. Somewhat easier times were seen when numbers were growing in the postwar period, and in the 1970s the university was given resources to meet the target of ten thousand students then set by the University Grants Committee. But in 1981 came financial cuts for the whole university system, felt particularly severely in Aberdeen with its deliberately inflated staff

*108 The offshore oil industry offers many subjects for research by university economists, engineers, geologists and geographers, marine scientists and medics, and even historians.*

108

numbers: the university was faced with an immediate cut of 23 per cent in its grant. In the decade which followed, many individual members of staff took early retirement and some departments were closed and others amalgamated. Yet even in these very hard times, under Principal George McNicol whose arrival in 1981 had coincided with the UGC letter bearing the bad financial news, the university demonstrated its courage and resilience, and did more than merely survive a period of extreme tension.

Modest expansion in staff numbers and in courses taught had already begun in the interwar period, despite limitations of finance, and after 1950 both staff and courses expanded greatly. The arts faculty inherited from the nineteenth century had six professors and taught ten subjects. By 1980 the faculty of arts and social sciences had 26 professors and taught 21 subjects. Science expanded similarly, from four chairs to 23, and besides many varieties of the BSc in pure science, offered degrees in agriculture, forestry and engineering. Medicine went from seven chairs to 16, remodelled its curriculum to meet the changing needs of the profession, and introduced the medical sciences degree and a BSc in health sciences. Divinity added two more to its existing four chairs, and began to teach for the BD degree in 1924. Law had only one chair when the century began: it added five more by 1980, but also relied on part-time teachers drawn from the local legal profession, before but more especially after the introduction of the diploma in legal practice. Full teaching for the LLB degree began in 1909 - previously Aberdeen students had to take courses elsewhere to fulfil their professional qualifications. A degree of Bachelor of Commerce was introduced in 1919, but despite early promise it attracted few students after the economic depression of the 1930s, and it was abandoned in 1949. The financial crises of 1981 cut back the numbers of existing staff, but did not prevent new appointments being made and new subjects being introduced. Additions to the university's range of courses since then have included many varieties of environmental science; occupational medicine and ophthalmology; cultural history, European studies and women's studies; management and social research; agricultural business management and aquaculture; and a range of law and science degrees which incorporate European languages.

All these alterations over the century in staffing and in subjects offered opened a vastly wider range of choice to students compared with what had been open to them at the beginning of the century. That choice was further widened when the university modularised its undergraduate curriculum in 1990. As compared with the previous century, the other big change for students was the gradual swing away from the traditional Ordinary degree to the Honours degree, in both arts and science. By the 1970s a single or joint Honours degree had become the natural goal for the majority of students. Principal Sir Edward Wright made it a particular concern to ensure that Aberdeen's Honours degrees were fully equal to any offered elsewhere, and he saw his own son, after graduating at Aberdeen, go down to Oxford to take a higher degree, not a second first degree as so many Scots had done in the past. In and after his time, it was felt by many that the Aberdeen type of Honours MA or BSc degrees, taken over four years, offered a particularly attractive blend of breadth and specialisation. The changes which led from the Ordinary to the Honours degree as the norm for most students began with the new arts curriculum of 1909, which allowed more specialisation than formerly, and which was accompanied by a lengthening of the academic year. A fierce battle over the academic year opened in 1905 and raged until it was settled by the Ordinance passed three years later. The academic year had lasted from October to April, and though Aberdeen had already had a summer term this was then used only for teaching a few Honours students. The 1908 Ordinance brought in a three-term year of 25 teaching weeks and prolonged the session to the end of June.

Almost as fierce, though not so prolonged, were the arguments over the academic year in 1989, when the modular degree

*109 Students on a field trip in the Cairngorms.*

programme was grafted onto the three-term year. Throughout all the curricular changes, a continuing concern has been to favour breadth as well as specialisation within the degree programme. The older Ordinary MA had demanded a spread of courses which included philosophy, mathematics or a science, and a language (formerly Latin, later any foreign language). Even today a spread of subjects is demanded, though no single subject is compulsory. The tradition of breadth of study is also seen in the very wide range of Joint Honours degrees offered.

The move to Honours teaching had another implication. Whereas in the period down to the 1950s most teaching was done by means of lectures, thereafter small-group teaching became much more common. More informal connections between staff and students were developed, not only by this change, but by other things: field work trips; reading parties at The Burn or Tarradale House; the advisers of study system; academics in halls of residence. Relationships between different grades of staff likewise changed over time. When the century began, professors were the only people who mattered. They appointed their own assistants, who enjoyed no formal tenure and usually stayed for a maximum of three years. There was then only a handful of lecturers, appointed by the university to help in the largest classes or to institute the teaching of new subjects. During the century the numbers of lecturers has vastly increased so that they now outnumber professors by ten to one, and the growing emphasis on research has also led to the appointment of many research and technical staff. Library, administrative, secretarial and other staff have also increased

*110 A room of one's own is the great attraction of university residences, and a study-bedroom can soon fill up with friends. Nowadays the rooms are less austere than those described in the inventories of 1542 and 1634.*

110

greatly in number, to match the growing size of the university. At the end of the Second World War the university was still a small organisation of professors and their assistants. From the 1950s, it became increasingly a large organisation employing many kinds of staff, and, incidentally, one of the biggest employers in the North East of Scotland.

The growth of the student and staff populations, and the recruitment of numbers of academic staff who had no previous connections with the North East, meant that the university lost something of its previously intensely local character. Whereas in 1945 over half its students came from homes within 30 miles of Aberdeen, by 1975 that proportion had fallen to less than a quarter. Nevertheless, the university retained a strongly regional and Scottish character. In the early 1990s its undergraduate population was still drawn roughly one-third from the traditional catchment area of the North East, the Highlands and Islands of Scotland; one-third from the rest of Scotland; and one-third from elsewhere.

To house so many students with homes far from Aberdeen, the university had to build halls of residence. The local character of the university, and the tradition of students who were not at home living in lodgings, had left Aberdeen as the last British university to provide no official residence for students, other than some medical students. In 1960 it opened Crombie Hall, a hall for 46 men and 64 women students, probably the first such mixed hall in Britain. Typically of Aberdeen, the bold step towards co-residence was taken for financial reasons. It was

111

*111 Johnston Hall. Named after Secretary of State for Scotland and university chancellor Tom Johnston, this student residence was opened in 1966.*

calculated that a hall for women only would not pay its way, yet women more than men seemed to need residential accommodation. This admirable pragmatism led to a very successful experience for the university, which went on to build more such halls and flats, so that by the 1980s half its student population could live within easy walking distance of the main academic and recreational buildings in Old Aberdeen.

A large non-residential building programme was also needed as the university grew. This had already started before the Second World War to allow the re-balancing of teaching departments between Marischal College and King's, though the major achievements in extending the building stock came after 1950. The migration of science departments to Old Aberdeen began with botany in 1922, and by the end of the 1980s all engineering and all sciences, except those teaching preclinical medical subjects, had moved, most of them into handsome purpose-built academic premises in Old Aberdeen. The interior of Marischal has been continuously remodelled, at great expense, to meet changing teaching needs. This made it difficult, even when it might have seemed desirable, to withdraw altogether from the Marischal site. Instead the university reinforced its commitment by maintaining the Student Union building next to Marischal College.

The shift to Old Aberdeen was inexorable, however, because the university had more space there. It began in the 1920s to buy up individual properties in the Old Town as these came on the market and it also built on many formerly open spaces it owned or acquired. The major residential development at Hillhead of Seaton, with the adjacent university playing fields at Balgownie, involved the biggest acquisition of land. Besides the new science buildings, and the science library - later to be enlarged and transformed into the main, Queen Mother, library - striking buildings in Old Aberdeen included the New King's lecture rooms of 1912; the Elphinstone Hall of 1930, the Sports Pavilion of 1940 – one of the university's first 'modern' buildings – and the transformation of the King's College Library into a Visitor and Conference Centre in 1991. The development of the Old Aberdeen site has been architecturally sensitive, blending domestic architecture and institutional buildings successfully, and retaining beautiful garden spaces like the MacRobert Memorial Garden, the Senatus Courtyard, and the Cruickshank Memorial Gardens (maintained since 1898 for the teaching of plant sciences). In 1949 Principal Taylor promised that the expansion of the university in Old Aberdeen would not create an 'academic suburb': 'It is one of the attractive features of the present community that all types and classes live here.' That promise has been honoured, as the character of Old Aberdeen today shows.

The other major building project of the twentieth century was the creation of the Foresterhill hospital site, inspired by the vision of Professor Matthew Hay. By 1935 the Royal Infirmary and the Sick Children's Hospital had been built, and the Maternity Hospital almost completed, a project paid for by money collected locally. In all of this the university co-operated closely. To the new Foresterhill hospitals it added, in 1938, its own medical school building, which allowed clinical medicine to move out of its cramped space at Marischal. The new medical school was planned with shared lecture rooms and a single medical museum, instead of replicating the departmentally-based academic accommodation of the past.

Medicine is conspicuously a subject in which the university sought to serve its own region. The Aberdeen Royal Infirmary remains in the 1990s a specialist hospital serving a huge land

112 The Elphinstone Hall was built in 1930 to take over the functions of the old Great Hall (which had stood on the other side of the Cromwell Tower, but had been taken down to make way for the new library building of 1870). Designed for use as an examination hall, 'the Elph' was also used for dining and recreation. Dressed stone from the ruined Castle Newe on Donside was used in its construction.

113 On the lawn in front of the Elphinstone Hall, there stood until just before the First World War a large professorial manse. For some professors, until the mid twentieth century, a house that went with the job was a substantial attraction. The scale of this manse dwarfs the New King's teaching building in the background (opened in 1913) and must have rivalled in size King's College Chapel, beside which it stood. Professorial manses were not always as convenient as they were grand. Professor Milligan, who occupied the one just across the road from this, had to fight a long campaign with the Board of Works in the 1870s and 1880s to get a bathroom installed.

*114 King's from the playing fields shows a blend of old and new buildings. In the foreground is the Pavilion, opened in 1940, while just behind it can be glimpsed the Round Tower. To the right is the gable end of the 1870 Library, converted into the Conference Centre in 1991. The crown of King's, the spire of the chapel, and the top of the Cromwell Tower form the skyline of this picture.*

*115 Surrounded by beautifully restored domestic buildings, the MacRobert Memorial commemorates the three sons of Lady MacRobert killed between 1938-41 while serving in the Royal Air Force.*

*116 The Zoology Building, seen from the Cruickshank Botanical Garden. The garden was established in 1898 by Miss Anne Cruickshank to serve the needs of teaching and research in botany and to provide a public garden, both of which purposes are still realised today.*

117

*117 A patient arriving by helicopter at the Aberdeen Royal Infirmary. The hostile environment of the mountains and the North Sea provide casualties, but air links routinely bring in cases from all over the vast area of the North and the Islands.*

and island area, as well as the offshore world of oil exploration and production. One of the early commercial ventures in which the university became involved in the 1980s was the provision of off-shore medical services. Long before that the work of Sir Dugald Baird, in seeking to reduce maternal and infant mortality, not only helped very many individuals but demonstrated the importance of environmental factors for human health; more recently, the work of Sir Alistair Currie on programmed cell death has made a substantial contribution to the study of developmental biology and the progress of cancer research.

Local connections with research institutions in its area were of great advantage to the university. The Rowett Research establishment, with its many links with the university, was directed in the 1930s and 1940s by one of the most distinguished academics and public servants of this century, Lord Boyd Orr, who remained director when appointed professor of agriculture in 1942. His researches were the basis of Britain's food rationing system in the Second World War, and afterwards inspired the United Nations Food and Agriculture Organisation. Boyd Orr was awarded the Nobel Peace Prize in 1949. Equally practical in quite another field was *Mathematics*

118

119

*118 Sir Dugald Baird (1899-1986).*

*119 Lord Boyd Orr (1880-1971).*

*for the Millions,* written by Lancelot Hogben, professor of natural history from 1937 to 1941. Many distinguished natural scientists based their work on the rich environment of northern Scotland, and today the university is strong in such subjects as geography and land use, and in such applied sciences as soil science and forestry, which have obvious local relevance. Its faculties of arts and divinity have supplied much local talent, especially to the teaching profession and the churches, and music has always been shared with the city and the region. Social scientists have studied, among many other things, sparsely populated areas and the oil industry, as well as providing their share of graduates to serve the area. The local heritage has been preserved and interpreted by academics interested in Scottish history and literature and in Celtic, and the library has provided a regional resource of incalculable value. Extra-mural activity has taken the university message to the smallest villages and remotest islands of its region, and in the 1990s the Centre for Continuing Education is pioneering community-based centres of study using telephone and television links between students in Kirkwall or Stornoway and academics in Aberdeen.

The regional emphasis is, however, balanced by an equally strong commitment to national and international obligations and the worldwide work of scholarship and research. The very expansion of student numbers, which has been such a dominant theme of the university's history since the 1950s, was a response to government plans to expand the numbers of university graduates. Subjects such as botany, environmental science, soil science and forestry have indeed a special local relevance, but they have equally served the needs of India, Africa and the Far East. Medicine and divinity have continued in the twentieth century their contribution of trained personnel to serve at home and abroad. Aberdeen's remarkably strong connections with the British Empire from the mid nineteenth to the mid twentieth century were superseded after the 1970s by the renewal of older links with Europe, and the re-enforcement of a world outlook. Medical inventions, like that of magnetic resonance imaging, in which Aberdeen's department of biomedical physics was a world-leader, or the discovery of the enkephalins in the Unit for Research on Addictive Drugs, are obviously of universal significance. Professor J J R McLeod (physiology), shared with Banting and Best the Nobel Prize for Medicine in 1923 for their invention of insulin. Frederick Soddy, professor of chemistry 1914-19,

*120 The extraordinary conjecture in the mid 1920s that particles could behave as waves underlay a revolutionary new way of looking at atoms, called wave-mechanics. These Nobel prize winning pictures, produced by G P Thomson at Marischal College in 1928, show electrons diffracted by atoms in the same way that light waves are diffracted by cloud droplets to produce rings around the moon.*

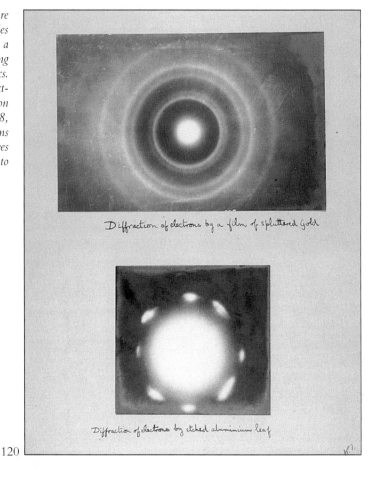

Diffraction of electrons by a film of sputtered Gold

Diffraction of electrons by etched aluminium leaf

120

won the Nobel Prize for Chemistry in 1921; and Sir George Paget Thompson, professor of natural philosophy 1922-30, began here the work which subsequently won him the Nobel Prize for Physics in 1937. These are examples of the ways in which the modern university has continued the intention of Bishop Elphinstone, to serve society and to serve truth.

*121 Old and new: the crown of King's reflected in the window of the Fraser Noble Building.*

# Acknowledgements

The authors acknowledge with deep gratitude the advice and guidance of fellow-members of the Editorial Board of *Quincentennial Studies in the History of the University of Aberdeen;* the work of past and current contributors to the series, on which they have drawn heavily; and the help and support of colleagues throughout the university.

Beyond the university, they are particularly grateful to Miss Marjorie Leith of Leith Editorial Services, production manager of the volume, and to Miss Mary Williamson for her timely survey of visual resources. The following individuals and institutions have graciously allowed the use of pictures in their possession: The Trustees of Blairs College (22); Aberdeen Incorporated Trades (32); City of Aberdeen Art Gallery and Museum (61, 62); The Natural History Museum (74); City of Aberdeen Library Services (79); Ms Diane Morgan (113); Aberdeen Medico-Chirurgical Society (118); The Rowett Research Institute (119).

Readers who wish to know more about the history of the university should turn to volumes in the Quincentennial Studies series, which embody the basic work of research and reinterpretation. Individual volumes in the series are available in bookshops; a complete list and order-form may also be obtained from the Sales and Publications Branch of the University Library. Another major work is Leslie J. Macfarlane, *William Elphinstone and the Kingdom of Scotland, 1431-1514* (Aberdeen University Press, 1985), which appeared shortly before the Quincentennial series began publication.